COACHING LINEBACKERS
AND
THE PERIMETER DEFENSE

COACHING LINEBACKERS
AND
THE PERIMETER DEFENSE

Gene Ellenson

Parker Publishing Company, Inc.   West Nyack, N.Y.

PRINTED IN THE UNITED STATES OF AMERICA

ISBN-0-13-139329-4
BC

Foreword

It is with warm pleasure and an honor for me to respond to Coach Gene Ellenson's invitation to write the Foreword.

I don't think anyone who has had the opportunity to play for and under the late General Neylan at Tennessee left without an understanding and an appreciation of the defensive game of football. In my 27 years of coaching as an assistant and head coach, I coached in all the areas of the game. However, I think I enjoyed most the defensive challenge. I have seen the game evolve from a simple single wing to the "T," split-T, multiple offense and the now popular pro-type offense. Through this evolution the defense was called on to defend one-third of the playing field in a single wing to the entire width of the field in the pro offense. Through this transition, more pressure was put on the defense with the major share of this increased pressure being put on the perimeter. In coaching the perimeter, more responsibility has been given in selection and training of personnel to play these positions.

This book is written by a close personal friend and one of the finest defensive coaches in the game. Coach Gene Ellenson has coached with pride and winning results all the defenses and the accompanying perimeter adjustments covered in this book. He has also brought you his own permanent innovations to the defensive game of football. You will find indepth coverage of this important area that has been given shallow treatment in most defensive publications. (I think the chapter on how to stimulate the mental as well as the physical approach to defensive football is worth the price of the book!)

With all the cycles in both offense and defense in the game of football, I think you will find this book one that will retain a prominent and permanent place in your library with more frequent and constant reference through the years.

A friend of mine who has been consistently a success on the professional golf tour gave me his philosophy for winning. He said you "drive for fun and putt for dough." I believe this philosophy could be applied to the game of defensive football. The pressing front play for fun, the perimeter and secondary play for the winning dough. Certainly no one will deny you cannot win consistently on the gridiron without a sound and well-coached perimeter.

In closing, I repeat a personal simple fundamental philosophy . . . "it is not what you know; it is what you coach."

RAY GRAVES
Athletic Director
University of Florida

What's in This Book for You

This is a book about football's toughest area of coaching and playing—linebacking and perimeter defense. Almost everyone is going to some defensive scheme that affords three linebackers instead of two, and in order to teach and coach linebacker play, one almost has to include the rest of the perimeter. The perimeter is the outside containment and deep containment of the defense. Specifically, these are the positions of defensive corner backs and twin safeties. Everything that happens on offense must happen inside this perimeter if the defense is to be successful. If you have a ruptured perimeter or leaky containers, you are going to get beaten.

The goal of this book is to cover the skills, techniques and responsibilities of the positions in the perimeter. The intent is to deal in specifics and not generalities. Every step, every move, every key will be covered in such a way that players, coaches, and future coaches will be able to benefit and improve by possessing this book.

There will be the big picture also. We will show how the individual skills and techniques fit into the overall scheme. Any coach can develop a defensive play book from this information. Each piece in the jigsaw puzzle is analyzed and then fitted together.

Here is a list of things the reader can look forward to learning in the following pages.

1. How to develop linebackers and secondary players from raw material.

2. Increase the number of drills and teaching methods related to defense.

3. How to stimulate the mental as well as physical approach to defensive football.

4. How to simplify recognition of offensive sets and motions.

11

5. How to build a goal line defense that you can count on.

6. Finally, a 4-3 play book that can be used verbatim. Every move of every player is detailed so that you could coach it directly from this book.

Offenses and defenses have periodically beaten each other. Every time the offense comes up with a trend, the defenses everywhere scurry around until they finally get this innovation stopped. Right now the offense is ahead of the defense. In the last few years the influence of the Pros on TV has brought about rising scores, and the average offensive gain per game has risen from 250 yards to 400 yards. Some teams are hitting close to 600 yards! This is great for the fans but defensive coaches everywhere are consuming more and more aspirin. Sooner or later the margin of victory will rest on a team's ability to defend.

This book deals with the problems of stopping the pro passing and multiple offensives being used today. There is a need for this because high school coaches are finding passers and receivers and putting their best athletes on offense. They are more or less letting the defense shift for itself. Most of these youngsters go to college, offense oriented, and it is difficult to find the good pass defender. This means defensive kids must be taught from scratch. It is hoped this book will stimulate some defensive thinking and create some athletes with defensive abilities.

I hope that the techniques and skills presented here will help coaches and players gain confidence in defense. Since defense is reaction, confidence is a great part of success. The plans must be sound and the execution automatic. It can't be automatic if there is any uncertainty or doubt. In short the plan *must work*. All we can ask of a young player is that he approach football with a "get wet all over" philosophy. That's what this book is all about—"getting wet all over" in regard to defense.

GENE ELLENSON

Contents

Part II

THE PERIMETER DEFENSE

Part III

THE GOAL LINE DEFENSE

Part I

THE LINEBACKER

1

Selecting the Right Player for Linebacker

Many successful coaches throughout the country think the most important thing that you will ever do is placement of your personnel. It is not an easy task, and there is always second guessing. If the truth were known, at least two-thirds of all staff meeting time is spent on shuffling the depth chart around. No one has a clear cut formula for instant success in this area.

The human element is involved and this increases error. Occasionally, a boy is not performing well at a certain position even though he has the "tools" so to speak. He gets moved to another position and suddenly he is a player. There are many reasons for this. Maybe it was what he wanted to play all along but never said anything about it. The most probable reason, however, is the manner in which he was "sold" on playing a new or different place. Confidence is everything. A coach should never say, "Joe, we are going to 'try' you at linebacker, etc." This is negative right from the start. A better way of making the change is to say, "Joe, I've been watching you and I *believe* you would make a natural linebacker."

Of course, this alone won't do it, but at least you are off on the right foot. It takes real skill in psychology to move a youngster to a position that he feels is stepping down in importance. For instance, moving a good sized fullback to offensive guard . . . or moving a tight end to tackle . . . or, and this one is the toughest, moving a quarterback to defensive safety. Not every kid has learned to sacrifice self for the good of the team, and it must be done in such a way that the player ultimately feels he made the decision himself and that it was not thrust upon him.

WHAT A GOOD LINEBACKER MUST DO

In this chapter we are dealing with the particular position of linebacker. The selection of personnel for this position on the defense should occupy the most thought and consideration of all positions. The reason for this is that usually the two top priority positions are quarterback on offense and linebacker on defense. Quarterbacks fall into their spot rather quickly since their talent is more noticeable. The selection of people to fill the linebacker position is more difficult.

You may ask why is the linebacker position *that* important? To answer, here is what a good linebacker must do:

1. Call defenses—he is a defensive quarterback.

2. Adjust defenses—quickly recognize offensive formations and make necessary changes using knowledge of scout report and game plan.

3. Be a tackler—linebackers must roam from side-line to side-line and must be their team's leading tackler.

4. Be a pass defender—they are the guts of the pass defense in the short areas.

5. Be a pass rusher—the terms "Red Dog" and "Blitz" always refer to rushing the quarterback and always involve linebackers.

6. Be a leader—a linebacker is the hub around which the rest of the defense revolves.

I made a season film study once about the breakdown of defenses. The results showed that for every running and passing play that gained five or more yards, the linebackers were the cause of the breakdown in 75 percent of the bad plays. After this study, we assigned a special coach to linebackers only, and spent a great deal more time in selecting and training this position.

I could list a lot of physical attributes that I would like to have in a linebacker. For instance, big, strong, fast, courageous, intelligent. But you can wipe all these things out if you find the one most important attribute—desire. Some kids just want to more than others. I don't mean to carry this to a ridiculous point. Certainly, a boy must have something going for him besides desire, but you must be open-minded enough to find that kid who really wants to do the job. Maybe a couple of short stories will prove my point.

One year when I was coaching the line at Miami Senior High School, we were having an "off" year and struggling to get by. Our big inter-city rivalry game with Edison was coming up, and we were plenty worried. Most particularly about our defense and linebacking. Our head coach, George Trogdon, told the backfield coach (Charlie Tate, later Head Coach at the University of Miami) and me to take our respective groups and come up with one kid each who would tackle somebody. We went to the practice field and went to tackling. Charlie found a 130-pound third-string blocking back named Schoen, and I found a kid only slightly bigger named Carnathan. These two kids came to the surface during this intensive drill, and we started them at linebackers. They had had no season-long training on linebacker responsibilities; they just wanted to tackle somebody. Well, we shut Edison out and won the game. Schoen and Carnathan were the stars.

"High School," you say, but that is what football is all about. College and pro football isn't that much different. Sure, training is important, but some other things are more important.

Let me give you another example. Here at the University of Florida we had a youngster named Steve Hiedt. Steve was a slow high school fullback. He only weighed about 180 pounds. He was the slowest kid on the squad by all our timing events. He never made the required mile run which we required of all players before the season started. Yet this youngster was our leading tackler on kick-off coverage. He wasn't a great linebacker, but in our most crucial game of the year against FSU he made the key interception that saved the game. Why? He wasn't big, he wasn't fast. All he did was get the job done.

Yet another quick example. A few years later we had another linebacker named David Mann. David was good sized—about 210 pounds and 6 feet 2 inches tall, but he was no sprinter. The best we ever clocked him was 5.2 in the 40 yard dash. We had many kids faster, but not many tougher. Anyway, we were playing Kentucky late in the season and preserving a narrow lead late in the game. Kentucky had an All-Conference back named Dickey Lyons, who was a true sprinter. Kentucky, on the last play of the game, through the use of motion was able to match Dickey Lyons against David Mann on man for man coverage. Lyons ran a flat and up route into the end zone. The pass was perfect, but our David Mann was right there running hip to hip with this 4.6 sprinter and broke up the pass. How can a 5.2 guy cover a 4.6 guy and not get beat? It can't be done you say. Well it can, if the guy is like David Mann.

Just one more story that has to go into this book about linebackers. One of the finest linebackers we've ever had at the University of Florida was Jack Card. Too small to get a scholarship, Jack came out for football on his own and earned a scholarship. He was 5 feet 6 inches tall and weighed 166 pounds! It just wasn't believable. We gave him a jersey with #1 on it because he just wasn't big enough to wear two numbers. And he didn't become just a squad man, he became a starter. He beat out a kid who was 6'4" and 225, who could move; in fact, the guy Jack beat out was drafted by the Dallas Cowboys! Jack was a marvelous player and our defense that year was 7th in the nation. Jack was our leading tackler with 90 unassisted tackles for the season. He was handicapped on pass defense because of his lack of height, yet he still managed a key interception of a Joe Namath pass the year we played Alabama.

These stories point up my main thinking about who should play linebacker. Somewhere on every squad is a kid who has enough physical ability along with that extra quality of being special. It is the hardest thing in the world to measure. Successful coaches just get a feeling about certain kids, and even though they are disappointed occasionally, more often than not, they are right.

HOW TO RECOGNIZE POTENTIAL LINEBACKERS

We must deal in this book about measurables. The rest of this chapter will deal with those things we can measure. Little things that may help you recognize some of the talents all good linebackers must have.

1. *Quickness.* You can notice this in anyone of a number of agility drills spelled out later in this book. Don't be deceived by straight away speed. It doesn't mean too much. In fact, great speed often produces a linebacker who will overrun plays and gets in positions to be cut back on.

2. *Football Smart.* For some reason, some kids are school smart and football dumb, and sometimes the opposite is true. I have had players who were in engineering school, but never understood what driving up underneath a curl meant. Conversely, I've had some who struggled in class, that knew where that curl pattern was without me telling them. Of course, we've had them smart in both areas,

but if a kid isn't football smart, don't play him at linebacker.

3. *Shuffle Ability.* This is hard to describe. It is hard to teach also. All I really know is that every good linebacker could "shuffle." I'll do my best to describe the technique. It is sort of a sidewise run that keeps the shoulders parallel to the line of scrimmage. It is not a cross over, it is just a short movement with both feet more in the manner of a dance step. The body is in a hitting position and the eyes are reading the keys like Liberace. The speed of this movement varies but it is just right to maintain leverage on the blockers and on the ball. More linebackers "over-pursue" than any other mistake. There is also something about the body attitude which is more alert than any other movement—you meet blockers better and you never over-pursue.

Another facet of shuffling is the "shuffle-in-place" or "bounce." When a linebacker is not sure of the point of attack he must just bounce or shuffle-in-place. There is an old coaching axiom that says "Never cross the offensive center fast." So when flow goes away from a linebacker he must shuffle in place or even shuffle back a little—then he shuffles to the line of interception with the path of the ball.

There are times—when the ball is out of his leverage—that the linebacker must turn perpendicular to the line of scrimmage, lay his ears back and run like the dickens to re-establish his leverage. But when he approaches his tackle, he must again get square to the line of scrimmage and shuffle into the tackle. If he is forced to make a last ditch angle tackle, somewhere along the line he didn't "read" the play properly and lost his leverage on the play.

4. *The "Hates to Look Bad Attitude."* This varies in all people, but I've noticed that the best linebackers are the kids that seem to suffer more when they have erred. Other kids accept failure to varying degrees but the kid I want backing up my line is the kid who can't wait to make up for his last boo-boo.

5. *Patience.* Patience by the coach and patience by the would-be-linebacker are necessary if you ever expect to bring the young player along. I hated to hear a coach get up in a staff meeting and say "so and so will never make a linebacker, or a player, at any position." Time and time again I've seen this proven wrong. A certain player may not be able to help you right now, but there'll come a day when you are glad you've got him. If you can find one little ray of light to keep a kid trying, you'll find the investment well worth while.

6. *Shows Up in the Game.* This is, I suppose, trial and error method of finding out who should play linebacker. I mention it because a lot of coaches put too much faith in drills. I've seen a lot of kids who look great in hitting drills but just seem to get lost in the "wad" during a game or scrimmage. You are going to play a game of football, not give an exhibition of drills. Therefore, the only place to make decisions is in game-like conditions. While I'm on the subject, all assistant coaches should get off the field on scrimmage days. All they do is get in the way and do the thinking for the player, which you don't want. You have to find out what the player will do on his own.

7. *Coachability.* This one is so obvious it's hardly worth mentioning. But the fact is, some kids are just easier to coach than others. Certainly you would want a linebacker who is coachable.

8. *Inquisitiveness.* Linebackers should be full of questions. "Why are we doing it this way?" is a damn good question. "Why can't we do it such and such a way?" is another. You might learn something. Questions indicate that the player is really thinking and linebackers have to think.

9. *Short Striders.* For some reason I've never had a good linebacker who was a long strider. Almost to a man, they ran with average to short strides. Along with this physical characteristic let me say that I never had a good linebacker whose feet toed out, or one that when standing straight bent back at the knees. Another peculiar fact is that none of them ever had bulging calf muscles. They were all, generally, trim-legged. The shorter ones were better tacklers and the tall ones better pass defenders.

10. *Football Nose.* Sooner or later every coach must admit that there are some things about linebacking that just aren't coachable. We call this talent "having a nose for linebacking." Some kids just seem to be able to smell a play coming.

You can get a reasonable job out of a kid if you teach him his responsibilities on the defense, and teach him to read his keys, but there are times when he must be right without the proper key. There is something about this kind of linebacker that makes him somewhat cautious. When you design a defense that calls for him to shoot the gap, he is usually a poor gap shooter. It is because his nose tells him not to commit too soon.

On the years when I had linebackers with real good noses, we simply didn't blitz much. Other years, with kids not quite so nose conscious, we blitzed more.

While I'm on the subject of blitzing, let me say that the best blitzers are kids that like to show off. Big noisy kids who like to show off make great blitzers. It is almost like pulling teeth to get a quiet, studious type to blitz.

In summary, let me tell you what I would do to pick my linebackers if I had no preconceived idea who they were. After three or four days of conditioning I'd scrimmage a game-type scrimmage with only one straight-up defense. Naturally, the offense would only have a couple of basic plays. Then I'd see who was making the most tackles *away* from his position. I'd get a list of kids that seemed to be the best pursuers. Then I'd eliminate according to the ten measurables listed previously above. I'd hope to come up with a couple of kids with good size, bright eyes, natural "quicks," trim legs, reasonable intelligence, pride in themselves, and that sensitive nose. Then I'd go about teaching them how to play linebacker—and that's what the rest of this book is all about.

2

Teaching Linebacker Fundamentals Effectively

HOW TO COACH STANCE AND AGILITY

The linebacker stance will vary depending on such factors as down, distance, and defense called. In general, however, a linebacker should be in a stance that will enable him to move quickly, see well, and meet blockers. The best way to describe it is that of a defensive basketball player guarding a man with the ball, only with the arms hanging down instead of one up, one down. Weight should be slightly forward on the balls of the feet. The feet should be staggered a little but not very much. The outside foot should be back in a 5-4 defense. The inside foot back in a 6-2 defense. The middle linebacker in a 6-1 or 4-3 defense can have a stance without a stagger. There should be a flexing of the knees and the body should lean forward just a little. The back is straight and the head is up. The arms are hanging straight down without rigidity and the hands are inside the knees. This stance will do the job for backing up the line anywhere behind the line.

Linebacker distance off the ball is usually two-and-a-half yards. Some linebackers are called upon to play the eagle, and some are called upon to play up on a tight end. In these cases the same stance applies except there is more flex in the knees, creating a lower stance. Also the position of the feet vary as to whereabouts you are playing the tight end.

In the "O" or outside position, the linebacker must stagger with his inside foot up. However, if he is threatened by a close wing he should change his feet and get down into a 3-point lineman's stance. If the linebacker is to play the tight end from the "H" or heads position, he won't have any stagger at all.

In the "I," or inside position, 4-3 defense, he will continue to

25

have his outside foot back but the opposite is true if he is an eagle linebacker. Eagle linebackers must be able to see the offensive tackle, therefore, they must have their inside foot back. See Illustration 1.

Teaching this stance can be done easily in a circle so the coach may see all at once. When working with the proper stagger, players should align on a "down" offensive lineman, and proper alignment checked; also depth off of the ball. Naturally, for short yardage situations the player is closer and for long yardage situations the player is deeper. Try to keep this thought in mind, the closer you get to the ball the lower you must get, and as you get farther away, the higher you must get.

This stance must be used in all drills henceforth. Some coaches call the position "breakdown" and will frequently, and unexpectedly, holler "break down" whereupon everyone assumes this hitting position—the linebackers stance.

AGILITY DRILLS

1. *Quick Around.* Players line up in single file about 6 to a group. The first man up breaks down, and on the hike he sprints ahead about 4 or 5 yards. At this point he drops his hand to the ground and runs around in a quick tight circle and out again.

2. *Dizzy Izzy.* Same drill as above only he keeps running in the circle until command of "ball" whereupon he sprints out of the circle.

3. *Grape Vine Run.* Just about every coach in America uses this running drill. It is a side wise running drill which calls for the trailing leg to alternate strides in front of, then in back of the leading leg. It calls for a good deal of hip turning and is excellent for a loosening up drill.

4. *Switch Running.* Players run backwards with legs pumping to one side; on voice command, whistle, or sight command such as moving a football from side to side, the player switches sides he is running on. He must never turn his back to the coach. Often the coach will throw a pass after several "switches" and the player must break on the ball and catch it.

5. *Zig Zag Sprints.* If you have a marked field to work on, you sprint the players, one at a time across the width of the field. The players run at 45 degree angles from one 5 yard line to the next as they go across the field. Each time they hit a chalk line they make

Front.   Side.

Normal Linebacker Stance

Illustration 1.

an *inside* pivot and go at 45 degrees back to line they started from. The fifty yard sprint calls for four or five pivots (Diagram #1).

6. *Wave Drills.* Two or more players face the coach. On the command "Break down" they assume the hitting position moving their feet quickly in place. The coach waves the football to the right and left, front and back. The players react quickly in the direction of the wave. The coach can include up and down also.

7. *Rope Drills.* Portable rope cages are easy to get and provide many drills for agility. They are elastic so there is no chance for injury. We didn't spend a great deal of time on this, but went through them every day. We went through straight, hitting every other hole, sideways hitting every hole, and crossed over hitting alternate sides and alternate holes.

8. *Over and Roll.* This is a tumbling drill using three men. All three face the same direction about a yard apart. They are on all fours except the end man who starts the drill by leaping over the middle man and rolling under the man on the other end. That man, of course, leaps over the roller and rolls himself under the remaining man who is now leaping. This continues as quickly as possible. You want to stress getting up off the ground as fast as possible in this drill.

9. *Run the Bags.* Place at least eight tall dummies on the ground lying flat. Defensive player must run through the bags sideways facing another player simulating a ball carrier. The ball carrier stops and starts, fakes, etc. The player running the bags must face him and stay in front of him without looking at his feet.

10. *Wind Sprints.* Good ole wind sprints. I've included this under agility because I feel we did something different along this line. Sprints are dull and painful. What you do them for is stamina. Normally boys won't push themselves to extend their stamina.

Then it occurred to us that everybody (including guards and tackles) like to run out for a long pass—the bomb. So at the end of practice I took the linebackers to an unoccupied section of the field. I got some B team and frosh quarterbacks and we heaved long passes at them without time to rest between sprints. Ten or fifteen of these were better than 20 or 25 half-hearted sprints.

WARD OFF DRILLS

1. *Half Circle.* One linebacker faces three other players cupped around him. All are in a hitting position. The coach stands behind

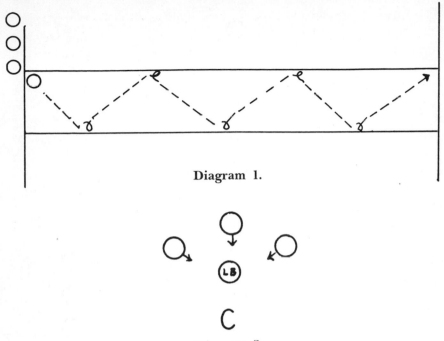

Diagram 1.

Diagram 2.

the linebacker and signals, either by pointing or voice command, which one of the three "blockers" will drive at, and stick a shoulder into, the linebacker. The linebacker meets this with his shoulder and flipper and bounces back into a hitting position again. The drill is done rapidly and the linebacker must move his feet quickly to meet the next "blocker." After six or seven good pops, rotate the players around until all have had a chance in the half circle (Diagram #2).

2. *Ricochet Drill.* One linebacker lines up in front of three blockers and a ball carrier lined up single file. He gets into a hitting position and wards off the three blockers one at a time. They come at him pretty hard, allowing time for each to strike a glancing blow and get out of the way. The second blocker should hit the opposite shoulder from the one the first blocker hit with. After the three good glancing blows, the linebacker keeps his hitting position and tackles the fourth man with the ball. He uses a "square" tackle putting his forehead right into the numbers. This drill can be done at half speed or three-quarter speed, it should not be done full speed (Diagram #3).

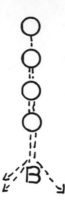

Diagram 3.

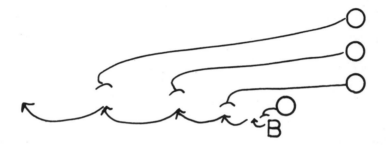

Diagram 4.

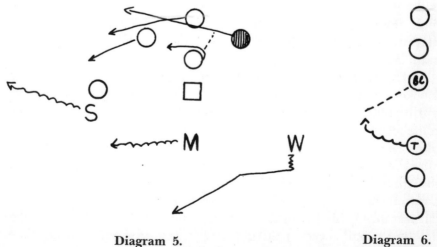

Diagram 5.   Diagram 6.

3. *Lateral Ward Off Drill.* The linebacker lines up in the "O" position on a tight end. Three blockers are also lined up in an "I" formation, behind where the offensive guard would be. On the "hike" the tight end tries to hook in, or "E" block, the linebacker, who uses a hand shiver to ward him off. The linebacker shuffles out as the three backs in the "I" come at him and throw blocks one at a time. The linebacker must play each one off and yet keep outside leverage (Diagram #4).

PURSUIT ANGLE DRILL

Linebackers Only. Set up a skeleton offense with tight end and three backs. Align linebackers in normal positions. The offensive backs run various actions and the linebacker coach checks each position to see if they are taking the proper angle, according to the defense called, to intercept the ball carrier (Diagram #5).

TACKLING DRILLS

1. *Angle Tackles.* This is a half-speed drill stressing position and form. Align two lines in single file with the two lead men facing each other at five yards. One line is designated as ball carriers and the other as tacklers. Players switch lines after every tackle. The ball carrier runs at a 45 degree angle about half speed. Tackler shuffles out, pacing him and goes into a "square" tackle lifting the ball carrier. It is not necessary to put the ball carrier down. After all have tackled, the ball carriers run at a 45 degree in the opposite direction (Diagram #6).

2. *Scramble Tackling Drills.* There are a number of these and they all stress the same thing—the ability to handle your body quickly and get into a tackling position. One that is used a lot is for the tackler and ball carrier to lie on the ground on their backs, head to head, about three yards apart. On the signal they both scramble to their feet. The ball carrier tries to get by the tackler and the tackler tries to tackle him. The same sort of thing takes place if they both do a forward somersault and then go into the tackle and run bit. Also two tacklers can get on their all fours and "ape" the ball carrier as he attempts lateral fakes and body rolls. When the ball carrier feels he has them out of position, he tries to run forward between them.

3. *Sideline Tackling Drills.* By placing a dummy about 9 yards from the sideline and making the ball carrier run a sweep and turn up in this area you can teach corner backs and linebackers to use the sideline in gauging leverage on the ball.

4. *Just Plain Full Speed Open Field Tackling.* This should be done with tackler and ball carrier no more than three yards apart. Draw parallel lines on your field three yards apart and ten yards long. The tackler stands on one line and the ball carrier faces him on the other line. The object of this "game" is for the ball carrier to reach the defenders line. He has ten yards laterally to maneuver in and wants to gain three yards or more. The tackler must prevent a three yard gain.

HAMBURGER DRILLS

1. *One on One.* Place two dummies seven feet apart. Use a football for alignment and, as in a game, pretend it is the neutral zone. One side is designated blocker, or offense, the other is defense. When the ball is pulled, the blocker tries to knock the defender out of the hole.

2. *Dummy One on One, Full Speed Tackling.* By adding a quarterback and running back to the above drill you can teach defensive stance, charge, release and tackling at the same time. By making the blocker passive you can really work on the defensive player.

3. *Hamburger Drill.* This is the combination of the two above drills. It should be done by everyone on the team. We used to take 10-15 minutes in the middle of every work day, and did this drill with five groups going at once. We put a quarterback and three or so running backs with each group. The offensive centers worked against the "Mike," or middle linebackers, the offensive guards worked against the defensive tackles, the offensive tackles worked against the defensive ends, the offensive tight ends worked against the outside linebackers, and finally the offensive wide-outs worked against the defensive backs (Diagram #7).

PASS DEFENSE POSITION DRILL

1. *Zone—Field Position Drill.* One of the hardest things to get execution on is zone position by the linebackers. They frequently forget where they are on the field in relation to the side line.

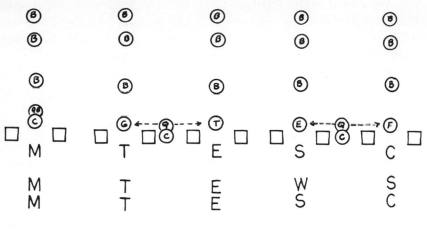

Diagram 7.

Start off with three linebackers on a marked field with the ball on one hash mark. Have a quarterback—only—establish the flow of the ball. Declare a strong or weak rotation and strength of the offensive set. Snap the ball and sprint the quarterback weak or strong or straight back. Check each linebacker to see that he is in the right zone.

Finally, the quarterback flips the ball somewhere near one of them and they all break on the ball. Then move the ball to the middle of the field and then on to the other hash mark. You want to stress where they go with relationship to the sideline. For instance, if you are the weak linebacker into the sideline, and rotation is to the field, you have the flat but don't have to go very far to get into the right position. However, if you were the weak linebacker into the field and rotation is into the sideline you would have a long sprint because that flat is a long one (Diagram #8).

2. *One on One Drills.* The best way to teach this is to work on one linebacker at a time. Use a skeleton offensive set up of four backs, a tight end, and two wide-outs. Run the various routes at the linebacker and show him how much cushion, etc. After a while he'll recognize routes and position himself correctly. Also you teach here the alternate procedure, should his man block. This usually is to look up the curl route by a wide-out and drive up underneath it.

That darn curl route against a man coverage is tough and that is why we don't want a weak linebacker covering a flat route close. If he'll keep leverage and get some depth, he'll be in the line of

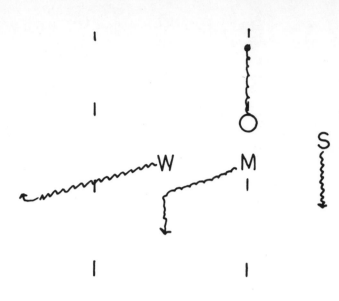

Diagram 8.

flight of the curl route, by a wide-out, and still be able to break up on the flat receiver.

Another reason for staying off a flat receiver is the possibility of him running a flat and up, and we want our linebacker to play the angles on this. When it is recognized, the linebacker must turn back to the inside and run with the receiver looking for the ball over his inside shoulder.

Working with the middle linebacker on this drill you'll find he's the most apt to have a second assignment and must learn to look for strong curls. "Mike" should also learn to belt people around, as most of his coverage is inside. The toughest thing is the second or third eligible clearing him deep to the inside, then the other one releasing short after a phony block. "Mike" should never have to cover more than 15 yards deep, then he can break back up on the delay route.

The strong linebackers problem is that usually he wastes time deciding whether to contain or fall off to the outside. We tell him this, "When in doubt, shuffle out." *Then* he gets his depth. He should get width first, then depth and, of course, look for the second or third eligible outside.

Break on the Ball Drills. Start out with your three linebackers standing in a row eight yards deep from the ball, about nine yards apart. Two yards behind and standing between them, place a stationary receiver. This makes four receivers standing in the "gaps." Throw the ball from seven yards behind the line of scrimmage to one of the stationary receivers and have the linebackers break on the ball for a tip or interception. It is also a good idea to have the middle linebacker be a step or two in front of the two outside linebackers to prevent them from having collisions. Next, keep the stationary receivers, but make your linebackers start out from their respective positions at the line of scrimmage. When the ball is snapped and the quarterback goes back, the linebackers sprint to their proper places and then break on the ball.

Catching the Ball Drills. Practice makes perfect and linebackers usually don't catch enough balls. We always started out each day with these few simple catching drills. The linebackers line up single file. The coach, or thrower, is about 20 yards directly in front. As the first man moves toward the thrower, a ball is thrown high where the linebacker will have to leap to get it. After all have had a catch at this, they break off to the right or left to catch lead passes. Finally we had a short tip drill. I found out the "tipper" could do a better job if he used a football to "bounce" the pass up into the air. One by one the linebackers break on these "bounced" passes and try to catch them at the highest point in the trajectory they can.

Shuffle Drills. The best drill to teach shuffling is often called "the eye opener." Place five big dummies on their sides about 4 feet apart. Have a line of ball carriers and a line of tacklers. The linebackers are defending each hole and the ball carriers are allowed to fake change direction but ultimately run in one of the four holes. This makes the linebacker shuffle and stay square to the line. Also he makes a square tackle and not one on the angle.

Recognition and Key Drills. These are really where a linebacker learns his responsibilities. Here again we need an offensive skeleton set up. Use your opponents sets. Start out with your strong linebacker who keys the second eligible (usually the tight end) and the flow. Run sweeps with hook-in and stand up blocks, run leads with turn out blocks, run a guard pull and trap, and run the off-tackle with the near-back kicking him out. He will learn to recognize what to do by the tight ends action. Any time the tight end doubles down, the strong linebacker closes laterally and keeps his outside leg free, forcing the ball outside. If the tight end, or near back, tries to hook him in he uses the hand shiver ward off drill technique. Also with this set-up we will call different defenses where the linebacker blitzes and still must play the same blocks.

Then go to the middle linebacker and work on him. He will be in one of his techniques such as inside, outside, etc. (explain later in Chapter 8). He keys the third eligible on the inside technique and must fill either side of his two tackles. On the outside techniques he adds the center to his keys as he must now fill first inside. We now run traps, and hand-offs at him. He must meet the center cut off, drive blocks and the fold and the slip by the guard.

Now we progress to the weak linebacker and he keys the fourth eligible. Run traps, hand offs, options, etc., at him. He must meet drive blocks, lead blocks, and crack back blocks.

This drill is what he must do in a game. We also mix in draws and passes. This is time consuming so you must allow time in your practice schedule to get it all in. Without this kind of work your linebackers won't improve and won't know the whole idea of their part in the defense or game plan.

3

Establishing Linebacker Techniques for Different Defensive Schemes

Linebackers are the most moved-around players in football. Every time a new defense is designed, or during-the-game adjustments are made, it is always the linebackers who get the brunt of the change. There is no way to record every odd ball defense in football.

To me, there are six major defensive schemes in football. At one time or another I have gone through a season with each of these schemes. They are: the 4-3 and 4-4 defenses, the 5-4 and eagle type, and 6-2 and split 6 idea.

This chapter will be devoted to teaching the techniques of each one of these major schemes. Techniques and responsibilities are very closely aligned. It is impossible to teach one without the other. But to highlight the differences in techniques, I am going to keep one central overall plan of pass coverage, strength declaration, set identification, hole numbering, eligible recognition and overall terminology. It may seem surprising but all these six different defenses can be taught around one basic plan.

The first thing I'm going to do in this chapter is to explain this general overall plan and then go into each defense separately. The 4-3 will be the first and most thorough, as it is the most popular, and will remain so as long as the pro influence continues to come into the colleges and high schools. This will also set many techniques and responsibilities which will overlap, or be similar to, those of the other defensive schemes.

HOLE NUMBERING FOR ALL DEFENSIVE SCHEMES

Every defensive scheme should number the offensive holes. These are the "Points of Attack" and all linemen and linebackers on

37

defense have a particular first responsibility. Since there is flip-flopping on defense to make learning easier, the holes should always be numbered from the strong side to the weak side. Therefore, those who always line up on the strong side (or weak) will have the same number holes to be accountable for (Diagram #9).

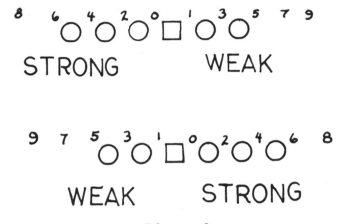

Diagram 9.

DECLARING STRENGTH

It is desirable to flip-flop the outside linebackers and the safeties. This means one linebacker and one safety learn only the techniques and responsibilities of the strong side and one linebacker and one safety learn only the techniques and responsibilities of the weak side. Also there are player types that fit these positions better. By that I mean, some players can do the things a strong linebacker must do better than they can do what a weak linebacker must do and, of course, vice versa. There are times when flopping should not be done. When faced with short yardage or goal line situation, I have never liked taking a lot of time in alignment. Their duties aren't affected by strength in these situations anyway. The rest of the time it is important.

To declare strength you have two basic considerations; the offensive set, and lateral field position (wide side—short side). We have just about eliminated field considerations except where there is no strength declared by the offensive formation. For example, if the offense lines up in a balanced set, such as dead T both ends tight, we will call strong to the wide side of the field. If the ball is in the middle of the field, we will declare a strong left on the idea that percentage tells us most teams are right handed. A coaching point here is that if the formation is dead T, but has one split end, the strength is now away from that split end.

There are only three formations that are balanced, dead T, double wing, or full I formation. Everything else has a strength factor. To us, any back set out of the backfield will indicate strength that way. In most cases today the tight end will show strength immediately, because almost every one has a tight end and a split end. The only time this varies is if the flanker sets in a slot to the split end side.

Now with these considerations at hand, it is fairly easy to declare strength. You soon began to realize the tough ones to declare.

Suppose the offense puts a flanker to the tight end side, but also puts a slot man to the split end side. This is a "Red Set" with us and we would declare it strong to the tight end-flanker side. "Red" doesn't have any special meaning except it tells us there are 3 eligibles who can get deep quick, because there are no defenders playing directly on them. The 3 "loose" eligibles would be the flanker, the slot man, and the split end. You see, a Red set *could* have two backs and an end lined up wide to one side, because three eligibles can still get deep quick. Naturally, we would declare strength their way.

As soon as the offensive team breaks the huddle, the strong safety and strong linebacker quickly "read" the set and call out "strong right or strong left." They do this as they, themselves, are proceeding to their own alignment position. Naturally, the weak safety and linebacker take up their correct positions.

NUMBERING ELIGIBLES

Now that we know where the offensive strength is, we immediately count the eligible receivers. Starting with the widest eligible to the strong side as #1, we count back to the weak side until all 5 have been counted. If a corner back is concerned only with #1 and #2, he doesn't count any further. This is true with all the positions in the perimeter, they locate the "key" that affects them. Of course, if we were going into a zone, counting doesn't become important. After doing this for some time, and seeing all sets, players know where all the eligibles are.

There could be some confusion when backs line up in an "I," shift, or go in motion. To properly count these sets, let's look at the "I" first. Since everyone uses just two backs behind the quarterback, we are now talking about #3 and #4. To be completely accurate we must consider the front back to be both #3 and #4 depending on which way he goes *after* snap. The tailback in the I is also #3 and #4 until he declares after snap. If they split, the one coming strong is #3 and the other, going weak is #4. If they both go strong together, then the front back is #3 and the tailback is #4. If they both go weak, together, then the front back is #4 and the tailback is #3. You should be able to see this correctly in the diagrams below. Anytime the offense uses shifts or motions, we simply count them where they *end* up. Don't try to change on fly (quick motion) because there just isn't time.

For instance, the offense lines up in a normal pro set. The tailback is #4. He goes in motion strong to the wide flanker. This makes him #2 and changes the tight end to #3 and the fullback to #4. Perhaps the following diagrams will make this clear. There is one situation linebackers must be wary of. When #3 and #4 cross after snap, they change and #3 becomes #4 and #4 becomes #3. This means that if you were the weak linebacker assigned to cover #4 and #4 crossed with #3 then you would cover #3.

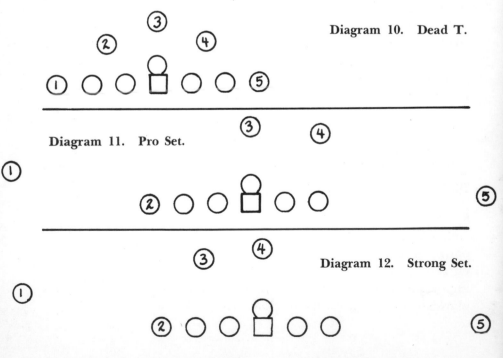

Diagram 10. Dead T.

Diagram 11. Pro Set.

Diagram 12. Strong Set.

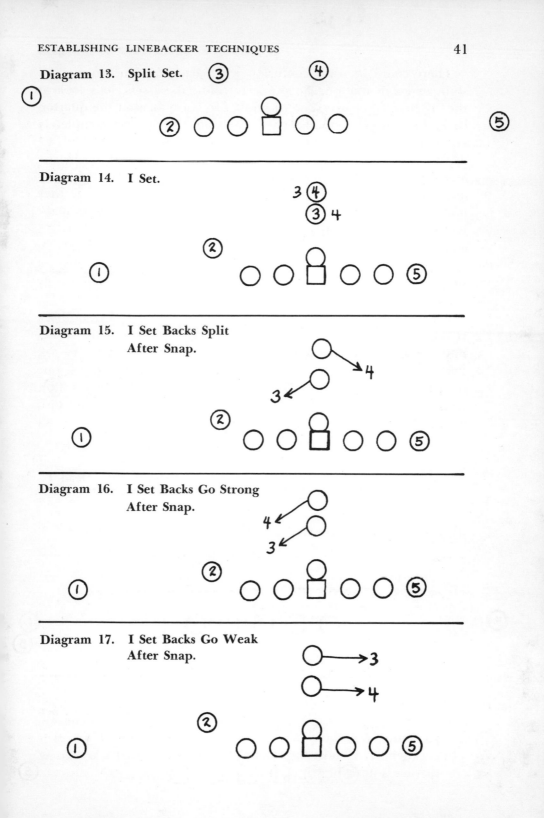

Diagram 13.   Split Set.

Diagram 14.   I Set.

Diagram 15.   I Set Backs Split
After Snap.

Diagram 16.   I Set Backs Go Strong
After Snap.

Diagram 17.   I Set Backs Go Weak
After Snap.

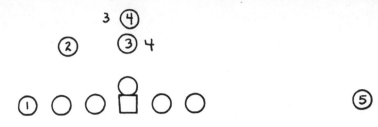

Diagram 18.   Power I.

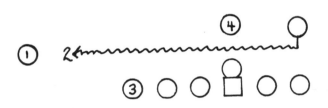

Diagram 19.   Pro Set Strong Motion.

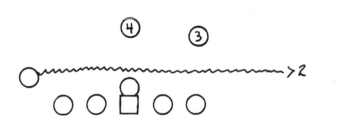

Diagram 20.   Pro Slot Cross Motion.

NOTE: This is the only motion that changes strength; therefore, you must renumber after motion man gets out of his own backfield. It is most important that the weak linebacker know that he is now the strong linebacker.

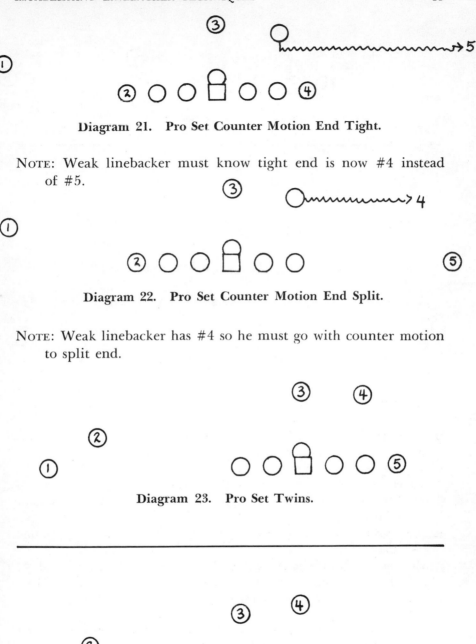

Diagram 21.   Pro Set Counter Motion End Tight.

NOTE: Weak linebacker must know tight end is now #4 instead of #5.

Diagram 22.   Pro Set Counter Motion End Split.

NOTE: Weak linebacker has #4 so he must go with counter motion to split end.

Diagram 23.   Pro Set Twins.

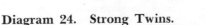

Diagram 24.   Strong Twins.

Diagram 25.   Split Set "Red."

Diagram 26.   Trips Set "Red."

More of this is explained in Chapter 6, "Identifying Offensive Sets."

BASIC TERMINOLOGY FOR ALL DEFENSIVE SCHEMES

Sam—Strong side linebacker.

Mike—Middle linebacker.

Will—Weak side linebacker.

Strong Corner—Corner to strength of the set.

Weak Corner—Corner away from strength of the set.

Strong Safety—Safety to strength of the set.

Weak Safety—Safety away from strength of the set.

Combo—Inside—Outside zone coverage by a corner and a safety on the two outside eligibles.

Sambo—Inside—Outside zone coverage by the two safeties on the #2 and #3 eligibles.

Banjo—Inside—Outside zone coverage by Sam and Mike on #2 and #3 eligibles. Also the strong safety can play a Banjo with Sam *or* Mike. In short, a Combo with a linebacker or two linebackers playing a Combo.

Bakerman—Man to man coverage by Will on the #4 eligible with no free safety. For example, on a Sambo call, Will would play Bakerman.

Red Set—Any time 3 offensive eligibles are set in such a way that they can get deep quick.

Forceman—Defensive back responsible to play wide run or take the "pitch" man on options.

You—Me—Call made by safety to corner telling him who the forceman is.

Him—Call to Sam backer telling him to be forceman.

Switch—This is a call given to the defensive end by the linebacker which places the end wide enough to contain. The linebacker must now take the ends run responsibility.

Second Back Out—Any back coming out of the backfield after the nearest back has released for a pass. Example would be #4 becoming a pass receiver to the strong side or #3 becoming a receiver to the weak side.

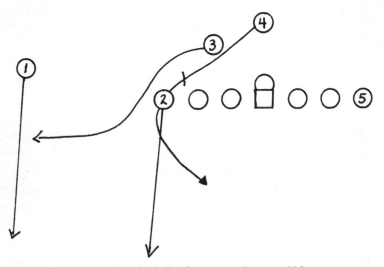

Diagram 27. 2nd Back out to Strong Side.

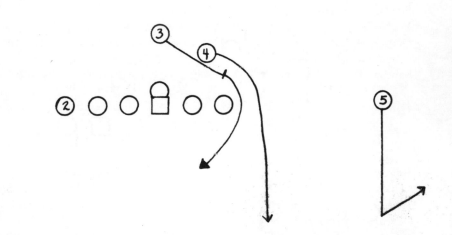

Diagram 28. 2nd Back out to Weak Side.

43 TECHNIQUES AND RESPONSIBILITIES

Mike Techniques of Play

A. STANCE

Use the stance as outlined in Chapter 2. The feet should be without stagger.

B. ALIGNMENT

Head on center, two yards from ball. Coaching Point—Don't get up inside the tackles feet.

C. KEY

"43 INSIDE"—Key #3. First responsibility is the 2 and 3 holes. "43 OUTSIDE"—Key the center and #3. First responsibility is the 0 and 1 holes.

D. CHARGE

Step with near foot first quickly to hole responsibility dictated by the key.

E. TECHNIQUES 43 OUTSIDE

Coaching Point: 43 Outside and 43 Inside are techniques that enable two tackles and one middle linebacker hold down the area from offensive tackle to tackle. On 43 Outside the tackles take the 2-3 holes after snap and Mike takes the 0 and 1 holes (Diagram #29). On 43 Inside the responsibilities change (Diagram #30).

Diagram 29.

Diagram 30.

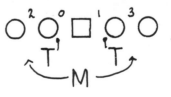

Diagram 31.

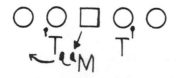

Diagram 32.

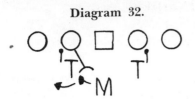

Diagram 33.

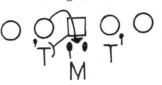

Diagram 34.

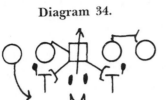

F. MIKE TECHNIQUES, 43 OUTSIDE

1. Center Cut Off Block (Diagram #31).
   (a) Step near foot in direction indicated by centers head.
   (b) Bring opposite foot parallel.
   (c) Keep blocker off your outside leg.
   (d) Locate P.O.A. and take proper pursuit route.
2. Guards Angle Block (Diagram #32).
   (a) Step to block quickly with near foot.
   (b) Hit with near shoulder and flipper.
   (c) Keep leverage and slide against pressure.
   (d) Locate P.O.A. and pursue.
3. Guards Fold Block (Diagram #33).
   (a) Centers key will tell you to step "up" with near foot.
   (b) You will now see guards pull. Bring other foot up parallel.
4. Middle Trap Technique (Diagram #34).
   (a) Centers key will tell you to step "up" with near foot.
   (b) Bring other foot up. Meet guard with outside foot, shoulder and flipper if trap is on you. If trapper goes on to trap your tackle, keep pressing ahead. You will make it impossible for offensive tackle to swipe you beyond the hole because you are already filling it. Be in position to tackle.

G. MIKE TECHNIQUES, 43 INSIDE

1. Guards Slip Block (Diagram #35).
   (a) #3 key should pull you in the proper direction. Keep square and shuffle out.
   (b) If guard has position on you, you were slow reading #3. You should beat him across and have your outside leg free.
   (c) If you don't have leverage, you escape by coming in behind the guard or pivoting around him.
2. Tackle Blast Block (Diagram #36).
   (a) Shuffle quickly on #3 key.
   (b) Use same technique as versus guards slip block.

Diagram 35.

Diagram 36.

H. NEUTRALIZING AND ESCAPE TECHNIQUES (applies to all three linebackers).

1. Hand Shiver. Drive both hands forward, striking blocker with butt of hands. Keep arms flexed, and follow through with body weight (Illustration #2).
2. Forearm Flipper. Drive forearm forward, upward, and use opposite hand to control blocker (Illustration #3).
3. Hand Grab. This is a hold technique. With both hands grasp blocker's jersey and firmly hold him away from your legs and body (Illustration #4).
4. Spin or Pivot. When shut off completely from your intended pursuit route, or when you've lost leverage on a blocker, you can regain position by pivoting off outside foot (or inside foot, depending on the use of an outside pivot or an inside pivot) throwing opposite leg, arm, and back into blocker. When you come out of spin you should be back

Illustration 2.

Illustration 3.

Illustration 4.

Illustration 5.

Illustration 6.

Illustration 7.

parallel to L.O.S. and have regained leverage (Illustration #5).

5. Slide.

Step laterally with outside foot and shuffle to P.O.A. using hands or flipper to keep leverage (Illustration #6).

6. Throw.

After using Hand Grab, throw blocker beyond you or away from P.O.A. while you step toward P.O.A. (Illustration #7).

7. Pursuit.

After escaping blocker, take the proper path that will enable you to intercept the ball carrier while preventing a cut back.

Sam Linebacker Techniques of Play

A. STANCE AND ALIGNMENT

Use stance outlined in Chapter 2. Sam has 3 basic positions on a tight end. "O" or outside position. The inside foot should split the middle of the tight ends stance "H" or Head on. Sam is eye-ball to eye-ball with the tight end. Feet parallel. "I" or inside. This will come up when tight end flexes more than 2 yards. The outside foot is back and inside foot is forward. Sam is at a slight angle towards the flexed end. See Diagram #37.

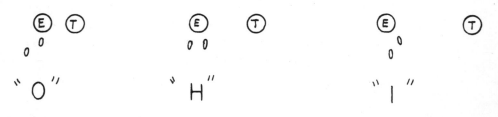

Diagram 37.

B. KEY

Tight end and #3. Sam has the off tackle hole, this can be either 4 or 6, depending on end's block. Sam has to force the quarterback on options and contain sprint outs.

C. BASIC CHARGES (Diagram #38)

"O"—Jab step with inside foot and bring outside foot up.

"H"—No charge, read.

"I"—No charge, read.

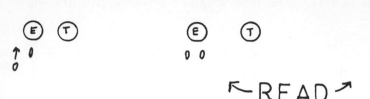

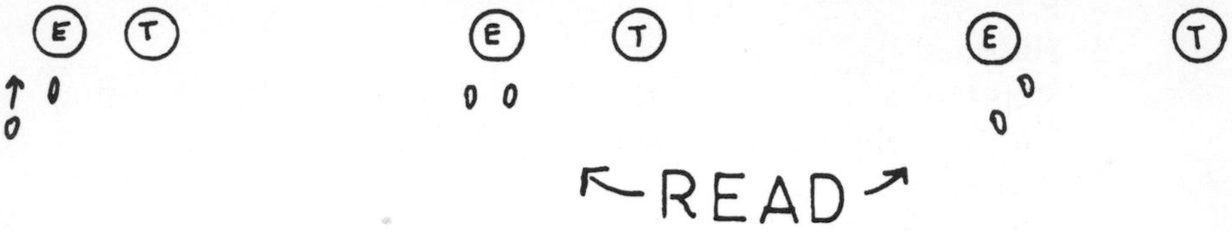

Diagram 38.

D. ATTACK TECHNIQUES AND REACTING TO RUN KEYS

1. Ends Stand Up and Wait Block (Green Bay Sweep) (Diagram #39).

   Use hand grab and force backwards. Do not commit inside or outside; buy time.

2. Ends Hook Block (Diagram #40).

   Use hand shiver and slide laterally moving with outside foot first. Keep end away from your outside leg.

3. Ends Turn Out Block (Diagram #41).

   Use inside flipper to keep end out of your middle body area and drop step with inside foot. Keep driving to the inside.

4. Ends Power Block to Your Inside (Diagram #42).

   Jab him off stride and shuffle to the inside keeping square. Be ready to meet the kick-out block from the near back or a pulling guard. Keep him from an easy release to your inside. Force ball carrier outside.

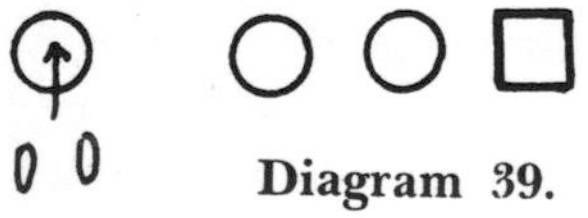

Diagram 39.

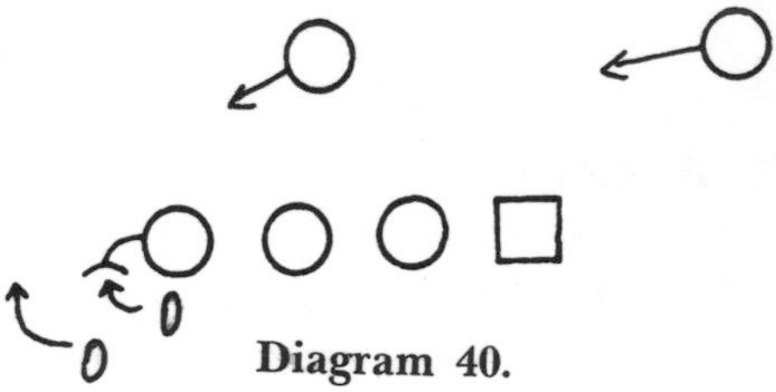

Diagram 40.

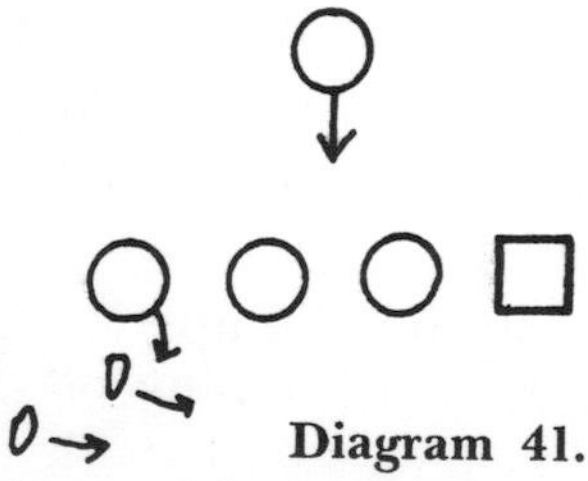

Diagram 41.

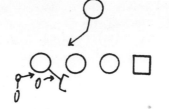

Diagram 42.

5. End Release.

    If the end tries to release outside, keep him off your outside leg and "flatten him out." This means make him continue wider than he wants to. You do this by shuffling out with him. Since you will have the outside of a combination coverage with Mike, this will put you in the right place. If the end tries to release inside of you, knock him off stride and be ready to shuffle out. If there is an inside release and flow of ball goes away, pursue back of line ready for counters and cutbacks.

6. Neutralize and Escape Techniques.

    These are the same as outlined under Mike techniques. You will meet more inside-out blocks than Mike and must do two basic things. One, keep your outside leg free, and two, stay square. Square means keeping your shoulders parallel to the L.O.S. You must be able to keep this position even though you must jab step and flipper the inside-out block. Never turn to the inside. This is called the "Catch" position and all you will do is catch the blocker.

7. Playing the Option.

    There is a basic rule about who forces the quarterback and who takes the pitch man on all option plays. The first man out—on the defensive line of scrimmage—who is not in a double team position forces the quarterback. The next man outside of him takes the pitch man. This means someone on the defense is positioned so that he is not flanked by an offensive blocker. It is reasonable to assume he can successfully make the quarterback pitch the ball. The next man outside of him may be a corner back or strong safety. Whichever one is not driven off deep must be the man to take the pitch. Players who try to drive both the strong safety and the cornerback deep by releasing the tight end and the flanker must be played a little differently. By scraping off the Mike linebacker you can force the quarterback with him. This leaves Sam to flatten out the tight end and take the pitch. Most of the time Sam will be on the quarterback, however. Sam should shuffle inside when he sees the tight-end block down. He should stay "square" looking upfield. As the quarterback approaches him, he should remain static. If he doesn't commit, and the quarterback doesn't pitch, they will collide. When the quarterback pitches (and he will) Sam is now in a square, or lateral position, and he can now break laterally out the line of scrimmage. This should give him an interception point with the runner, right on the L.O.S. When this technique is used Sam can often play both the quarterback and the pitch. He should get help from either the corner or the safety. If they are playing a blocker, at least they can turn the play in, which makes it even easier for Sam to catch the play. See Diagram #43.

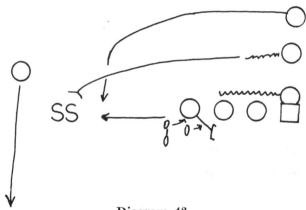

Diagram 43.

8. Containing the Sprint Out.

This isn't placed under the pass responsibility of Sam be-cause often it is a run defense. Sam plays his keys. He has seen the end release. He sees #3 sprinting at him with the quarterback going deep behind. All this time Sam keeps shuffling out. When in doubt, shuffle out. When it is obvious that #3 intends to block him and that the quarterback is not going to pull up, Sam must now drive up field keeping outside edge on #3 and make the quarterback pull up and throw. Sam uses the hand shiver and outside-leg-free technique. If #3 ducks inside and starts a pass route and the quarterback pulls up, then Sam, who has been shuffling out and has his width, now gets *depth* and covers #3. If #3 runs a route and #4 has come strong, as a blocker, ahead of the quarterback, and the quarterback continues to sprint out, then Sam must come up-field and contain as before. The fact that #4 has come strong relieves Sam of pass responsibility. This offensive maneuver has created an automatic Sambo and the safeties now play #2 and #3 receivers (Diagram #44).

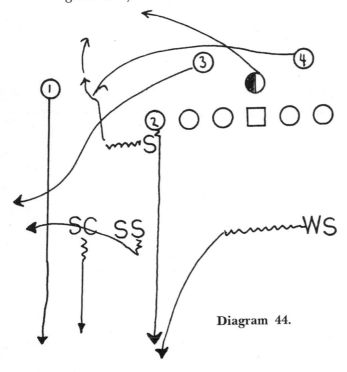

Diagram 44.

9. Neutralizing the Crack Back.

Sam can tell if he is going to be faced with this block by the width of the flanker or #1. If he is six yards or less, the possibility exists. Sam still keys the end but must use peripheral vision to know if he is meeting a crack back. He is square so he should be in a hitting position. Also Sam's corner back should warn him if #1 starts in on him. Any code word will do; we used "Crack" and it alerted all linebackers.

10. Keying the Slot Back.

Sam will often find himself faced with a slot back instead of a tight end. If the slot back is wider than 5 yards, Sam should "walk off." This is a position off the L.O.S. between the wide outs and the rest of the formation. Most of the time Sam will now cover and key #3. If the slot back is less than 5 yards, Sam should align on him and key on him the same as if he were the tight end. Slot back or not, he is still #2.

Will Linebacker Techniques of Play

A. STANCE

Same stance as outline in Chapter 2.

B. ALIGNMENT

1. Versus a tight end on the weak side you have the same alignment rules as Sam—(O-H-I).

2. Tight Alignment.

Normally Will will be on the split end side. Tight means he aligns head up the offensive weak tackle, two yards off the ball. Will can do this automatically if he is faced with an I formation or strong set. Also he can do this if he has the short side of the field on his side (Diagram #45).

3. Regular Alignment.

Will's normal position is two yards outside his end and two yards deep (Diagram #46).

4. Walk Off.

This position is two yards off the line and splits the distance between the offensive tackle and the split end (Diagram #47).

5. Double Position.

Will is called upon to double cover #5 and to do so he must align out on this wideout. The best position for double covering is to align just inside the wide receiver (#5) on the L.O.S. This takes away the look-in and all inside quick cuts. Will must key #5 and has the responsibility of covering him short. He must also see the ball and after he harasses #5, he drops back into a zone and plays the ball. If a weak side run develops, he comes back up and becomes the outside force man (Diagram #48).

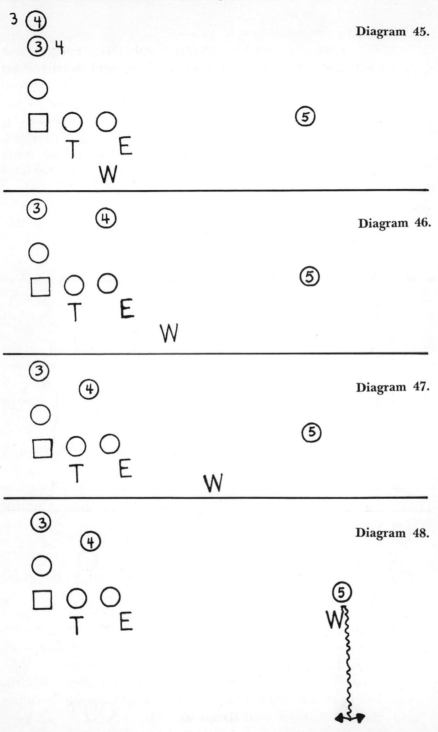

Diagram 45.

Diagram 46.

Diagram 47.

Diagram 48.

C. KEY

Will keys #4 in all positions except the double cover position. #4 will lead him to his run responsibilities and usually is his man to cover in a pass situation.

1. Tight Position.

Will always has an "in and out" game with his end. This is not a blitz but only defines which hole each is covering. Will has the 3 hole when he has given his end an "out" and has the 5-7 holes if the end is doing an "in." See Diagram #49.

2. Regular Position.

Will continues to work with his end and Key #4. See Diagram #50.

3. Walk Off Position.

Will must give his end an "in" anytime he walks off (Diagram #51).

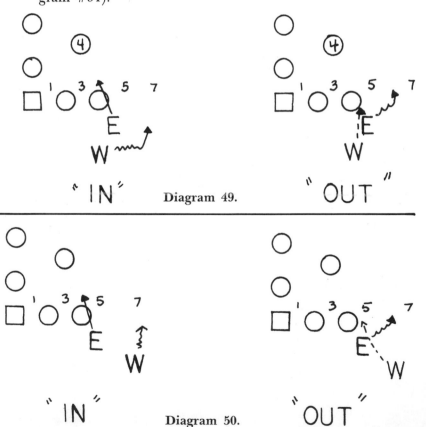

"IN"   Diagram 49.   "OUT"

"IN"   Diagram 50.   "OUT"

D. CHARGE AND ATTACKING THE BLOCKER

1. Tight Call, End Out.

Use your key. If key is your way, delay, then fill with inside foot first to a position inside your end. Will must force QB on options. If key is your way and a pass develops, keep leverage on #4 and cover him. If key goes away, shuffle back then pursue on proper angle if it is a run. If a pass develops and #4 is away, you will already be shuffling back. Keep going straight back and fill the area between your weak safety and cornerback. You can locate eligibles that may come into this zone. By practice you can pick up the dangerous route. Mostly you are there to prevent #5 from running a "break" or "post" route on your corner. See Diagram #52.

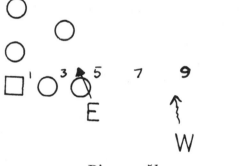

Diagram 51.

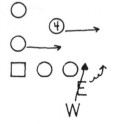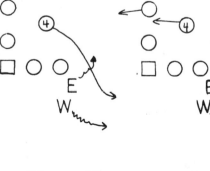

Diagram 52.

2. Tight Call, End In.

Key #4 if key is your way, shuffle out as you read run or pass. Versus run, Will must come up field aggressively and become outside force man and has the pitch on options. The other keys are the same as when in the tight position except that there's always the 5-7 holes for run responsibility. Will continues to have #4 on all passes. See Diagram #53.

3. Regular Position End In or Out.

The same responsibilities exist in this position.

4. Walk Off Position.

No charge. Play pass first. You have all outside responsibilities. Coaching point: always keep offensive tackle in your vision if he pulls, get upfield fast as the quick toss is coming (Diagram #54).

E. NEUTRALIZE AND ESCAPE

Will uses the same techniques as described earlier for Mike and Sam.

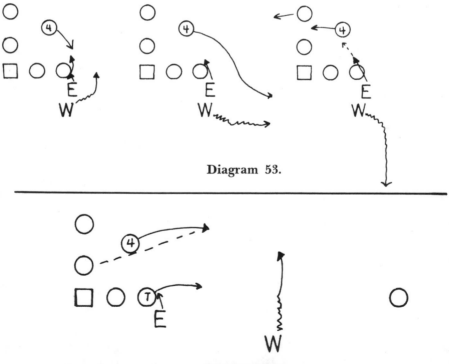

Diagram 53.

Diagram 54.

Blitz Rules for 43 Linebackers

A. SAM-WILL BLITZ—(FIRE 1)
1. Sam.

Versus a tight end align in the "O" position, and come hard on a line through the outside hip of the tight end. Use progressive blocker keys. End first, near back next, and inside-out block last. Use a hard charge to put pressure on the offense. This is a "contain" pass rush. Sam has the pitch on options. This is a "him" call and the strong safety must support inside of Sam. Use your keys to determine if blocks are inside-out or outside-in. If they are inside-out, set with shoulders parallel to L.O.S. and force runner outside. You must close the 4 hole. If the block is outside-in, play the blocker with a hand shiver and keep leverage on the blocker and the ball.

If Sam is faced with a flexed end he should call for a "cross" with his end. The end goes *first* and assumes the responsibilities of outside, option pitch, and pass containment. Sam assumes the end's responsibilities and must close the 2-4 holes.

When executing a Sam blitz, Sam must be wary of phony blocks by backs and read screen. When this happens, Sam must break off his charge and shuffle out laterally covering the screen man. He will have help but "screen" is everybody's responsibility. See Diagram #55.

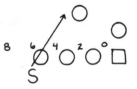 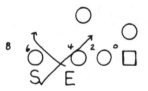

Diagram 55.

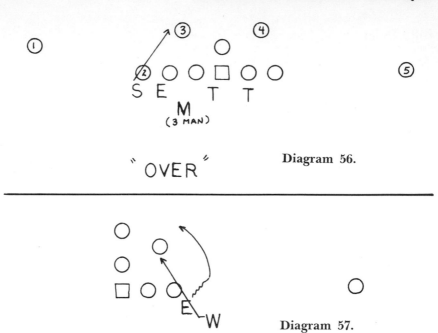

Diagram 56.

Diagram 57.

2. Mike.

Use regular keys. Mike has #3 man-to-man all the way.
If #3 is aligned as a half-back to the strong side, Mike must
call an "over" to his tackles so that he can move to a heads
position with #3. Mike must learn this on all Sam-Will
blitzes. See Diagram #56.

3. Will.

Use either tight or regular alignment and give your end
an in or out. This time Will comes hard on the snap through
the hole indicated by his "game" with his end. Versus a
tight or flexed end Will's rules are the same as Sam's. See
Diagram #57.

B. MIKE-WILL BLITZ—(FIRE 2)

1. Sam.

Align in O-H-I positions according to formation. Use regular keys. Sam has #3 man to man.

2. Mike.

Align in normal position, do not tip off the blitz. On the
snap, you will charge a gap predesignated. (Could be any
gap as long as it is co-ordinated.) For example, let us assume

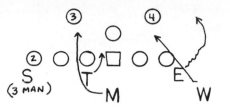

Diagram 58.

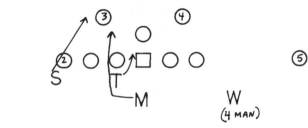

Diagram 59.

it is the 2 hole. Mike hits the 2 hole running and must not be late. He hits the gap with his shoulders square and is ready to change directions if he needs to take a pursuit route to the ball. If it is a pass he must get to the passer.

3. Will.

Use same technique as on a Sam-Will blitz. See Diagram #58.

C. SAM-MIKE BLITZ—(FIRE 3)

1. Sam.

Same as Sam-Will Blitz—(Fire 1).

2. Mike.

Same as Mike-Will Blitz—(Fire 2).

3. Will.

Use regular keys. Versus pass Will plays "Bakerman" which means cover #4 all the way. See Diagram #59.

D. WEAK SAFETY BLITZ—(FIRE 4)

1. Sam.

Same as Mike-Will Blitz—(Fire 2).

2. Mike.

Basically the same rules as a Mike-Will Blitz but he should blitz the "0" hole.

3. Will.

Same as Sam-Mike Blitz—(Fire 3). Will plays "Bakerman."
See Diagram #60.

E. STRONG SAFETY BLITZ—(FIRE 5)

1. Sam.

Your rules depend upon where the plan calls for the strong
safety to blitz. If he blitzes inside our end, then Sam is the
same as Mike-Will Blitz—(Fire 2). If he blitzes outside our
end, Sam must work an inside-outside game with the strong
safety.

2. Mike.

If the strong safety blitz is outside, Mike has his regular
keys and covers #3 man the same as Sam-Will Blitz—(Fire 1).

3. Will.

"Bakerman." See Diagram #61.

PASS RULES FOR 43 LINEBACKERS

(See Chapter 7 for definitions of color code regarding pass
coverages also motion rules are covered therein.)

1. Sam

(a) *Blue Coverage.* Use your regular keys to determine run or
pass. When you read pass you will play a "Banjo" with Mike.
This means you will cover #2 or #3 to the outside. If both
#2 and #3 release outside, Sam covers the widest of the two.
If they both release inside, Sam covers the nearest of the
two. While it is expected that Sam will cover either of these
two all the way, he will get help deep by the strong safety.
See Diagram #62.

There are some things that will change this coverage. If
the offense lines up in a wide slot (or twins), Sam and Mike
now have only #3 to play "inside-outside." The same would
be true if the offense got two wide-outs on the same side by
motion. See Diagram #63.

Sam also will have to contain the quarterback if he sprints
or bootlegs his way. A sprint out creates an automatic "Sambo."
The strong safety now takes #2 and Sam is free to contain. Sam will not have to contain a sprint or bootleg if the

Diagram 60.

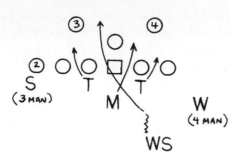

Diagram 61.

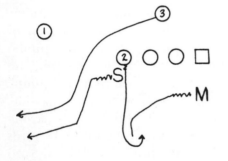

Diagram 62.

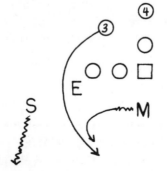

Diagram 63.

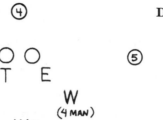

end is split on the strong side. The strong end can use a stand-up technique and contain this play. See Diagram #64.

Sam's alternate coverage is always #1. If #3 blocks and #2 released inside, Sam should be getting his width and depth while this is going on. Since he has no one in his zone, he looks up #1 and gets "underneath" him. He must be sure that #3 is not delaying and then releasing on a pass route (Diagram #65).

There is another technique Sam should be taught. Anytime he is covering #2 or #3 in the flat he should stay well off (cushion) the receiver and stay ahead of him. For a certain time during the pattern he will be in the line of flight from the quarterback to #1 running a curl or break pattern. Even though he is playing man, to a certain extent he is playing zone (Diagram #66).

(b) *Black Coverage.* Sam will either be blitzing or he has #3 man-for-man. This coverage is used on all blitzes.

(c) *Gray Coverage.* Sam covers #2 man-for-man. On this defense the two corners and 3 linebackers cover the five eligibles man-for-man with both safeties free.

(d) *White Coverage.* This is a rotating zone and is declared after the offense lines up. The weak safety calls the direction of the rotation by the code word "Jumbo Right" or "Jumbo Left." These words came into use because at one time we called this coverage "jump coverage." We are going to "jump" a wide receiver either to the strong side or to the weak side. For communication we used the word "Jumbo." On strong jump (Jumbo to Sam) Sam has the hook zone up to 10 yards directly behind him. On weak jump (Jumbo away from Sam) Sam has the strong flat and has to sprint to get there. Bear in mind that Sam may have to break this off and contain a sprint out—unless the strong offensive end is split. See Diagram #67.

(e) *Orange Coverage.* This is a prevent defense and, simply, it is strong-jump executed.

2. Mike

(a) *Blue Coverage.* Mike reads his keys and determines run or pass. After pass has been established Mike plays Banjo with Sam and has #2 or #3 inside. This is explained above. Mike must always be wary of two possibilities. One, if #3 and #4

Diagram 64.

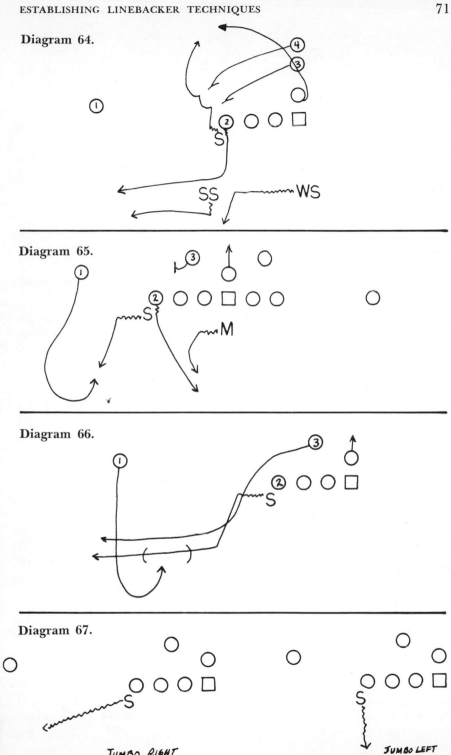

Diagram 65.

Diagram 66.

Diagram 67.

JUMBO RIGHT   JUMBO LEFT

Diagram 68.

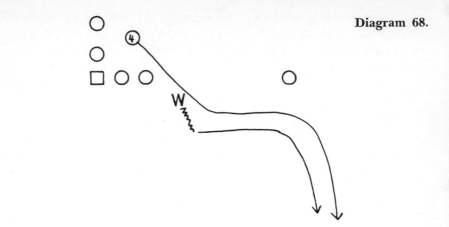

Diagram 69.

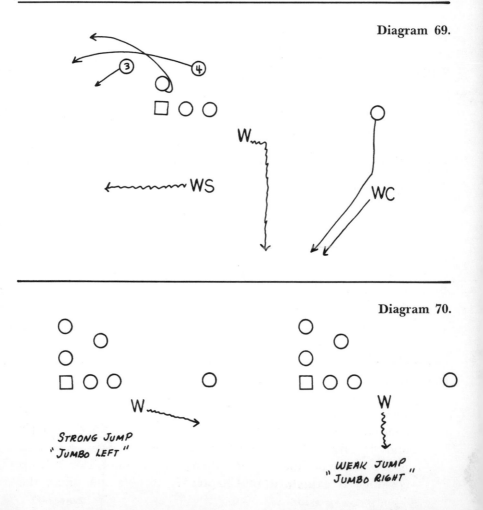

Diagram 70.

STRONG JUMP
"JUMBO LEFT"

WEAK JUMP
"JUMBO RIGHT"

cross in their backfield, #3 becomes #4 and #4 becomes #3. Two, Mike should be alert for #4 sneaking out to the strong side and #3 slipping out to the weak side. Coaching point: Mike should never go deep with #2 or #3. Either the strong safety or weak safety will help out deep. Mike must break back up on delayed receivers.

(b) *Black Coverage.* Mike will either be blitzing or has #3 man-for-man.

(c) *Gray Coverage.* Mike has #3 man-for-man. Note: Mike may have to call an overshift to get himself in position to cover #3.

(d) *White Coverage.* Jumbo Strong, Mike has the weak hook area up to 10 yards. Jumbo Weak, Mike has the strong hook area. In other words, Mike always has hook away from the jump or rotation.

(e) *Orange Coverage.* Mike has the weak hook area.

3. Will

(a) *Blue Coverage.* Will has #4 all the way. He may get help deep from the weak safety (who is free) or he may not. He must play #4 with cushion and be able to go deep with him (Diagram #68).

Will must also be alert for #3 and #4 crossing and be ready to pick up #3 coming to his side. If #4 blocks or goes strong, Will should shuffle back into the area between his weak safety and weak corner back. This particularly true when the offensive quarterback sprints strong, as the weak safety will go strong (Diagram #69).

(b) *Black Coverage.* Will is either blitzing or has #4 all the way because we have no free safety.

(c) *Gray Coverage.* Will has #4 man-for-man.

(d) *White Coverage.* Will covers the weak flat on strong jump and the weak hook on weak jump (Diagram #70).

(e) *Orange Coverage.* Since this is strong jump executed, Will goes out and doubles #5 before snap.

(f) *Special Coverages.* There will come a time when a "hot" receiver needs to be doubled, but you don't want to play zone all day. Also offensive teams will play him at #1, #2, and #5. By calling "Blue Coverage Double" you can wait to see where he lines up, and then play double 1-2 or 5. This coverage is explained in Chapter 7. It does not affect the

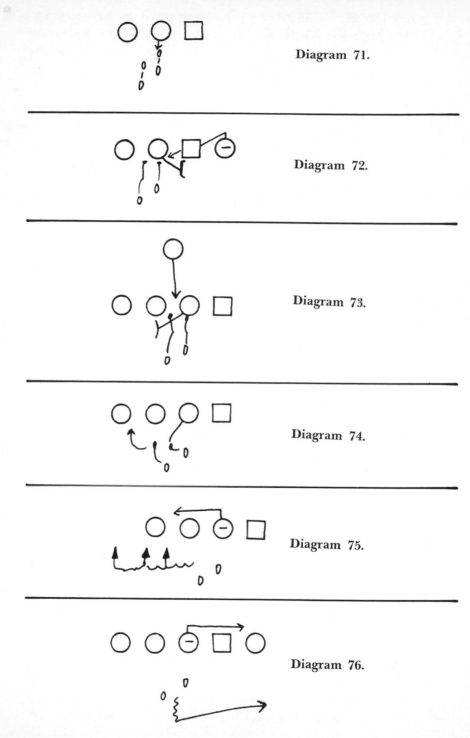

Diagram 71.

Diagram 72.

Diagram 73.

Diagram 74.

Diagram 75.

Diagram 76.

linebackers who continue to play Blue. There is one exception and that is "double 5," and Will must get out, before snap, and cover #5 short. The corner on that side has him deep.

54 TECHNIQUES AND RESPONSIBILITIES

A. DECLARE

Use declaring rules set forth earlier in this chapter.

B. STANCE

Use the stance set forth in Chapter 1, except a 5-4 linebacker should have a more pronounced stagger with his outside foot back.

C. ALIGNMENT

Outside shoulder of the offensive guard, two-and-a-half yards deep. You must be aware of offensive guards split from his center. The more he splits the closer to the line you must play and maintain spacing with your middle guard.

D. KEYS (Strong Linebacker)

Key the guard and the number #3 back. The guard is your first key. If he shows pass, you then pick up #3 as he is your man to cover. If #3 is lined up outside of you, you will have to go to a strong eagle. If #3 is lined up as a fullback and blocks, then your assignment is hook-curl. The guard remains your key on all run plays. The following rules apply:

1. *Your Key Blocks Straight on You.* Meet him with a two-step attack. Outside foot first, then hit with inside foot, shoulder and flipper (Diagram #71).
2. *Your Key Blocks Down.* Step up into line square and look for trapper (Diagram #72).
3. *Your Key Blocks Out.* Step up into line square and look for fold block by tackle or lead block from backfield. These blocks must be met in the hole (Diagram #73).
4. *Your Key Tries to Reach Block You.* Keep outside leverage and fill inside your end first (Diagram #74).
5. *Your Key Pulls Your Way.* Shuffle out parallel to line of scrimmage (Diagram #75).
6. *Your Key Pulls Across the Center.* Shuffle back then take proper pursuit angle (Diagram #76).

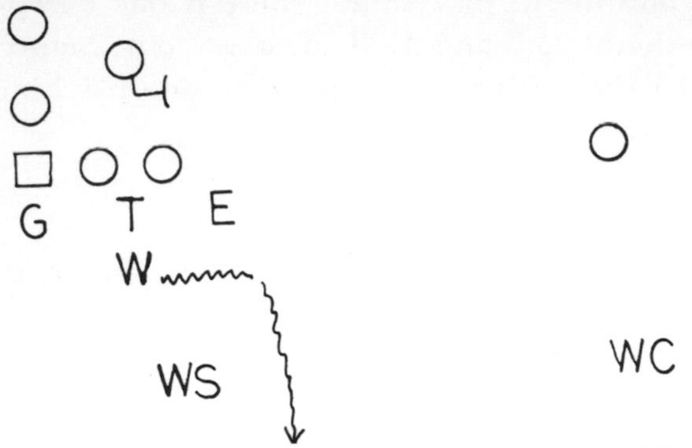
G T E
W
WS
WC

Diagram 77.

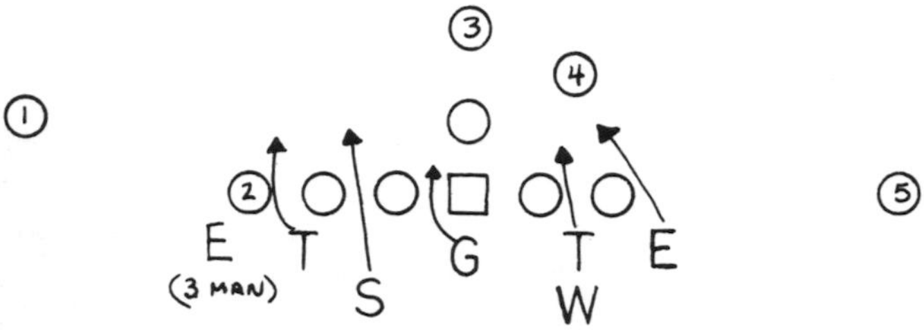
3
4
1
2
5
E T G T E
(3 MAN) S W

Diagram 78.

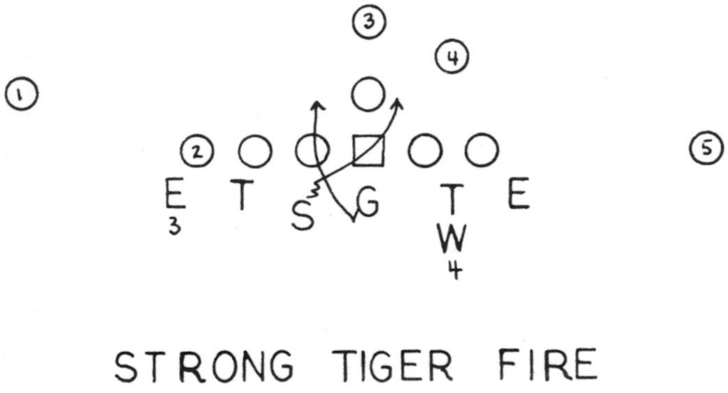
3
4
1
2
5
E T S G T E
3
W
4
STRONG TIGER FIRE

Diagram 79.

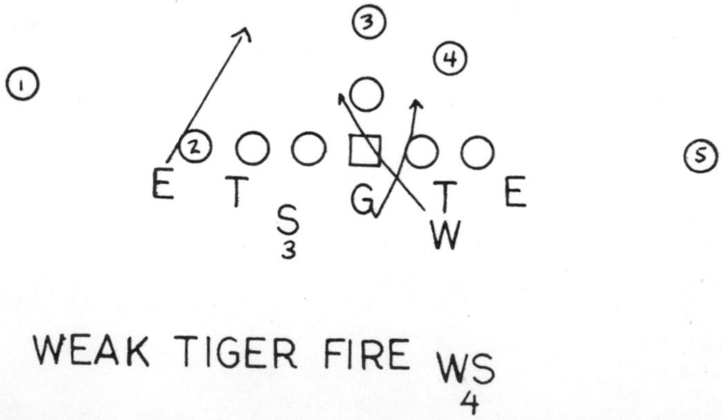
3
4
1
2
5
E T G T E
S W
3
WEAK TIGER FIRE WS
4

Diagram 80.

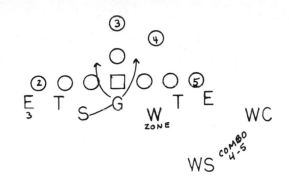

Diagram 81.

Weak Linebacker

Keys are the same as the strong linebacker as far as the running game is concerned. This is as long as there is a tight-end on the weak side. If the end is split, you will go into a weak eagle and key #4 for run and pass. If #4 blocks or goes strong, you back up and fill the area between the weak corner and weak safety if it is a pass. If it is a run, pursue on the proper angle (Diagram #77).

E. BLITZ RULES 54 LINEBACKERS

1. *Slant Fire.* SLB fires G-T gap and strong end covers #3. WLB same as 54 regular (Diagram #78).
2. *Strong Tiger Fire.* SLB cheats up and fires through center's position. MG crosses behind him. SE takes #3 and WLB plays regular. This stunt can be done to the weak side, then SE comes hard and WS takes #4 man to man. See Diagrams #79 and #80.
3. *Strong G Fire.* This is similar to the tiger stunt. The difference is that the middle guard comes strong and goes first with the SLB crossing behind him. This also can be done to the weak side (Diagram #81).
4. *Double Strong G Fire.* SLB does a slant fire and WLB and MG do a weak G fire. SE takes #3 and WS takes #4 (Diagram #82).
5. *Double Weak G Fire.* Same as above but to the weak side (Diagram #83).

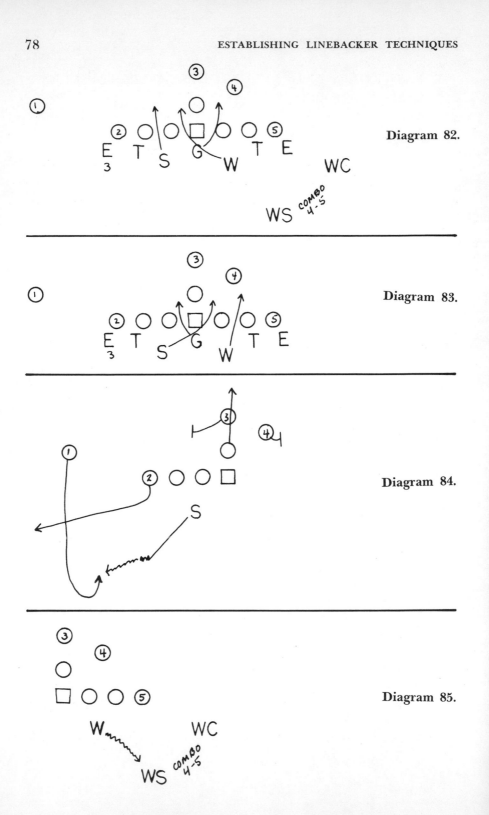

Diagram 82.

Diagram 83.

Diagram 84.

Diagram 85.

F. PASS RULES AND TECHNIQUES 54 LINEBACKERS

1. *Blue Coverage.*

    (a) Strong L.B.—When your guard key shows pass, locate #3. (#3 will be in the full back position because if he wasn't, he'd be in the near back position your side, and that would mean you would be in a strong eagle. Strong eagle pass rules are under "Eagle Techniques and Responsibilities.") If #3 releases, cover him. If #3 blocks, turn sideways to L.O.S. and sprint back to your hook zone 5 yards from your alignment looking for the tight-end hooking. If the tight-end does not hook (goes flat or deep) break laterally and look for the wide-out curling and get underneath the curl. It may seem that there are too many keys to read before the strong linebacker could get underneath a curl. Practice will speed this up. Also scouting, down and distance, and previous plays can be a factor in shortening the reaction time. For instance, you know you are playing a "curling" team—it is a passing down—or they've already hurt you on a curl. You wouldn't waste time reading run keys but would "play the obvious." When the offense gets you coming and going you will then have to take more time on recognition, but when your team is restricting the run well, you can align deeper and help more on the pass (Diagram #84).

    (b) Weak L.B.—Your rules are more pass oriented. You have #4 man and that means you'll be playing a lot of weak eagle. To keep from repeating, the weak eagle pass rules are under the next segment "Eagle Techniques and Responsibilities." There is a situation that should be brought up here. If the weak linebacker has a tight end, his side, he doesn't have to worry about #4 as the weak safety and corner back will have a "Combo" on #4 and #5. The weak linebacker then has "hook" only. See Diagram #85.

2. *Black Coverage.*

    (a) Strong L.B.—You will either be on the blitz or covering #3 man to man. Here again you may have to go into a strong eagle. In order to keep this system of coverages, your strong end must use the 4-3 "Sam" rules.

(b) Weak L.B.—You will either be blitzing or covering #4 man to man.

3. *White, Gray, Orange and Special Coverages.*
   (a) Strong L.B.—Same as Mike on the 4-3 defense.
   (b) Weak L.B.—Same as Will on the 4-3 defense.

EAGLE TECHNIQUES AND RESPONSIBILITIES

A. DECLARE
Same declaring rules.

B. STANCE
Basically the same as described before. The difference is in the feet and the amount of crouch. The feet are staggered with the *outside* foot up, and because eagle linebackers are on the line, they must crouch more (bend in the knees) to get lower.

C. ALIGNMENT
The outside foot (the up foot) is on the line of scrimmage and is even with the inside foot of the tight end.

D. KEY
The eagle linebacker keys the offensive tackle, but "feels" the end. Also if a pass develops, the eagle linebacker has #3 man for man or uses his alternate coverage if #3 blocks. (Explained later.)

E. CHARGE
The eagle linebacker jab steps into the end using a flipper and "feels" his block, if any. All the while he is watching the offensive tackle. He does not penetrate but stays on L.O.S.

1. End Blocks Down on Eagle L.B.
   Keep leverage on ends block and don't give ground. You have the off tackle hole (5 hole) first. Use slide or pivot (spin) technique (Diagram #86).

2. End Turns Out.
   No pressure from the end and you'll see what the tackle is doing. If he turns out on you, set square and meet him with inside flipper. Use same technique as Sam (4-3 defense) when tight end turned out. Keep leverage, drop step with inside foot and drive to inside (Diagram #87).

3. End Turns Out, Tackle Blocks Down.
   Set square and look for a lead block or trap. Penetrate toward the lead blocker and try to meet him in his back-

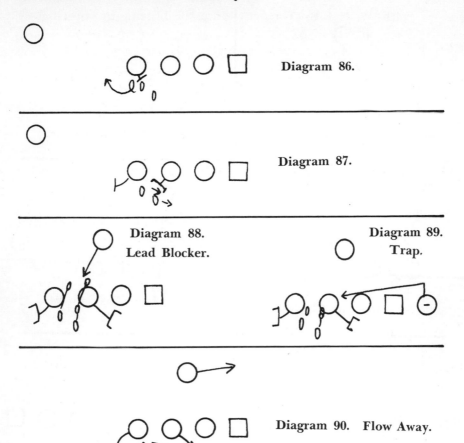

Diagram 86.

Diagram 87.

Diagram 88.
Lead Blocker.

Diagram 89.
Trap.

Diagram 90. Flow Away.

field. Shuffle laterally inside if end, tackle, and rear back are not blocking on you. Look for an inside out block from a pulling guard. Meet him with inside shoulder and flipper and keep square. If none of this happens, you will recognize flow away. Eagle linebackers pursue behind the line looking for cut backs and stay on an angle that will intercept the ball carrier. See Diagrams #88, #89 and #90.

F. EAGLE LINEBACKERS BLITZ RULES AND TECHNIQUES

1. Eagle Fire.

Strong linebacker versus a tight-end has the option of blitzing the tight-end—tackle gap or calling a cross charge with his end. It is important that he take the same alignment

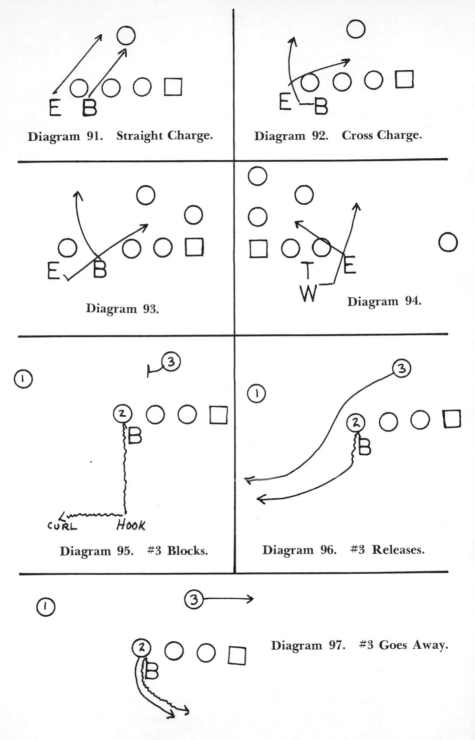

Diagram 91.   Straight Charge.

Diagram 92.   Cross Charge.

Diagram 93.

Diagram 94.

Diagram 95.   #3 Blocks.

Diagram 96.   #3 Releases.

Diagram 97.   #3 Goes Away.

as on his "reading" defenses so as not to tip off his moves. When blitzing like this, the strong linebacker and his end must work together. One of them (depending on the stunt) must be the outside force, contain, and take the pitch on options. See Diagrams #91 and #92.

Against a flexed tight end, the strong eagle L.B. should call for an invert cross. This means the L.B. crosses first (Diagram #93).

The weak linebacker's technique is the same as the strong L.B. if he has a tight weak end. If not, he will cross charge with his end from his weak eagle position (Diagram #94).

G. EAGLE LINEBACKER PASS RULES AND TECHNIQUES

Blue Coverage.

Strong linebacker—Your end releases and your tackle key shows pass, you locate #3. Start back with the tight end watching #3. If #3 blocks, you have "hook-curl." If #3 releases, pick him up and cover him. Use same technique as Sam on the 4-3 defense. Watch out for #3 and #4 crossing. If #3 goes away, pass show, don't let tight end do a "short across." Keep bumping him deeper and stay with him. See Diagrams #95, #96, and #97.

Weak linebacker—You have #4 on everything except when there is a weak tight-end and when #4 goes away. Versus a weak tight-end the weak eagle linebacker has hook only as #4 and #5 will be played by the weak safety and corner back.

Coaching points—When playing a true eagle on both sides, it is impossible to use the strong or the weak-end in the pass defense as it is necessary that they contain. This means the strong L.B. always has #3 and the weak L.B. always has #4. There is one way 4-3 pass rules can be used. That is to give the Sam rules to the Strong L.B., the Mike rules to the middle guard. Everything will fall into place this way, but it has been my experience that middle guards just aren't that versatile. It has never worked for me.

This means that you can't play Gray Coverage. It also means that on Black you must give up one receiver, usually #3. And on White and Orange, you must give up either a flat or a hook area. It is easy to see why so many coaches are going to a three linebacker scheme.

62 TECHNIQUES AND RESPONSIBILITIES

A. DECLARE

Use declaring rules set forth earlier in this chapter.

B. STANCE

Use stance as set forth in Chapter 1, except your *inside* foot is staggered slightly back.

C. ALIGNMENT

Both strong and weak linebackers align on the inside ear of the offensive tackles; however, the "wide side" linebacker may go to head up. Depth off the ball can be as deep as 3 yards depending on down and distance.

D. KEY

Both linebackers key the offensive tackles and the backfield action. They must be aware of the tackles block and the flow of the backs. They use the same techniques as 5-4 linebackers, the difference being in that the 5-4 linebackers key the guards and 6-2 linebackers key the tackles. There is another difference in that a 5-4 is an outside edge defense and the 6-2 is an inside edge defense. Basically, however, the moves, by key, are the same. If the offensive tackle blocks down or out, the linebacker must fill. If the offensive tackle blocks straight out on the linebacker they meet the block with a two-step attack and stay square. If the key shows pass, the linebackers go to their pass responsibility. On flow away the "off" linebacker shuffles back and then across keeping leverage on the ball. Remember on wide plays, the 6-2 linebacker pursues from the inside-out. He always is in position to take cut backs.

E. BLITZ RULES FOR 62 LINEBACKERS

There are only two logical places to blitz 6-2 linebackers. One is straight over the offensive tackle and the other is a cross charge with the defensive guards. There are other stunts but these two are the logical blitz places. See Diagrams #98 and #99.

F. 62 LINEBACKER PASS RULES AND TECHNIQUES

You can fit our "running theme" of pass coverage into a 6-2 situation but the most common pass coverage on a 6-2 is zone using the ends. As such then the basic coverage would be Orange.

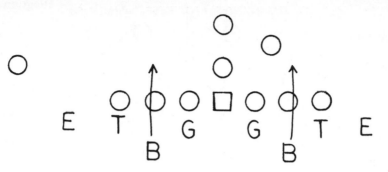

Diagram 98.   Straight Blitz.

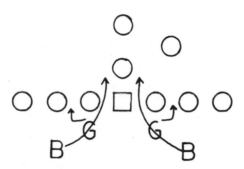

Diagram 99.   Cross with the Guards.

Orange Coverage

Both linebackers read pass using their keys. If the quarterback goes straight back, the linebackers retreat over their outside shoulders and have the inside hook zones. They pull up, square up and break on the ball (Diagram #100).

If the quarterback sprints out or uses play fake action, the linebackers have hook—flat. The key to which area they have is the quarterback action. When the quarterback starts his sprint, the defensive end has flat *until* the quarterback clears his offensive tackle. Then the end must come up field to contain. This means the linebacker doesn't release for the flat until he knows his end must contain (Diagram #101).

Diagram 100.

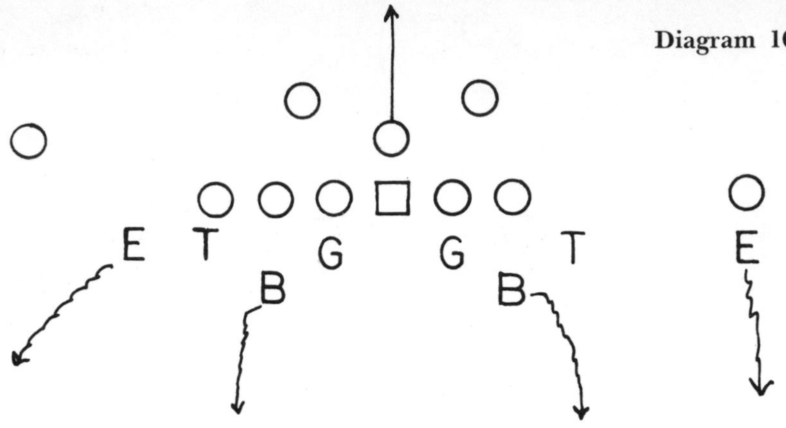

Diagram 101.

Diagram 102.

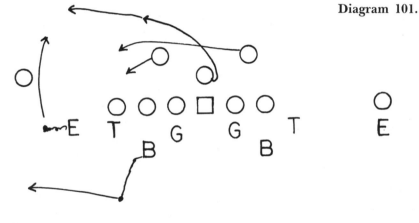

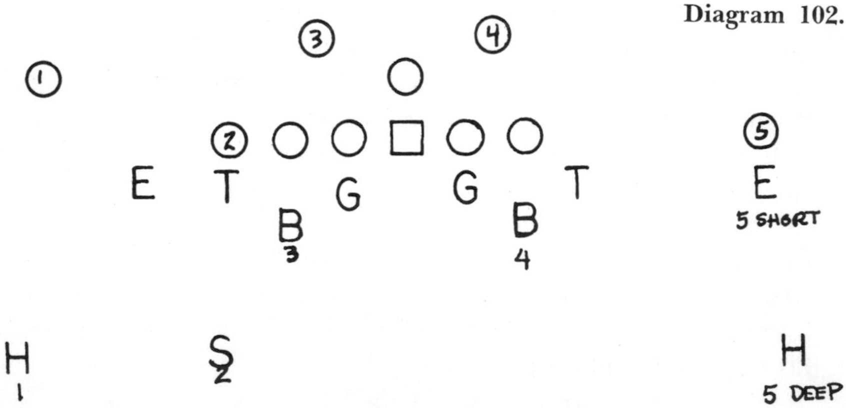

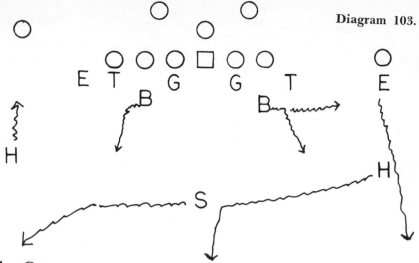

Diagram 103.

Blue Coverage

By squirming the safety over, head up the offensive tight-end, you can play a man type coverage. The strong H.B. and safety have #1 and #2. The strong L.B. has #3 man. The weak linebacker has #4 man. The weak halfback has #5 deep. On a 6-2 the defensive weak-end should double a split-end and take him short (Diagram #102).

White Coverage

You can cover the flat with the halfback but it means a full rotation and one end or the other is going to have to cover deep (Diagram #103).

Motion Rules

Wide tackle 6 linebackers are never affected by motion. The ends handle all motion by rotation or direct coverage. First of all 60 ends double any split-ends, so any motion to a split-end is covered by the doubler. On any counter motion the end to the side of the motion goes with the motion (Diagram #104).

On any other kind of motion the end to the side of the motion covers the motion man up to a depth of 10 yards and the other end rotates back to a 3 deep half back position. See Diagrams #105 and #106.

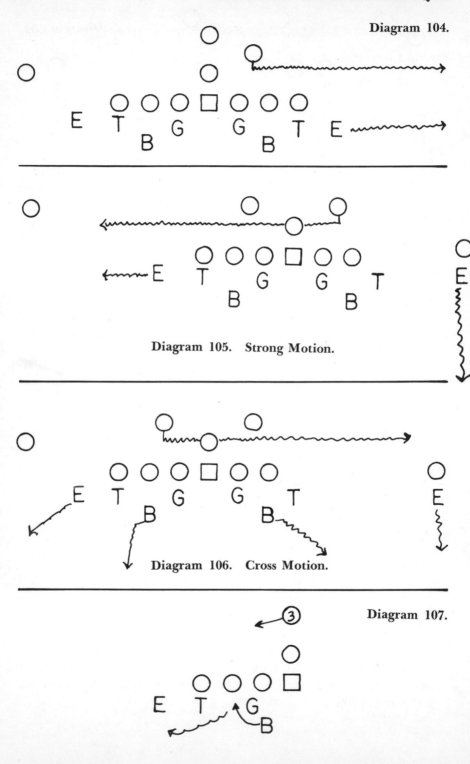

Diagram 104.

Diagram 105.   Strong Motion.

Diagram 106.   Cross Motion.

Diagram 107.

SPLIT 6 LINEBACKER RESPONSIBILITIES AND TECHNIQUES

Strong Linebacker

A. DECLARE
Same as set forth earlier.

B. STANCE
Same as set forth in Chapter 1 except the feet are square.

C. ALIGNMENT
Two to three yards deep, splitting the offensive guards inside foot. You can control offensive line splits by moving inside and up closer if the offensive guard takes a big split.

D. KEY
Basically the same as 4-3 keys. The strong linebacker keys #3 and the weak linebacker keys #4.

E. PLAY AT SNAP
- Strong Linebacker.
  Your key (#3) comes to your side, you must take area outside your guard first. If play goes wider, keep leverage on the ball by shuffling out (Diagram #107).

  Against a belly option take fullback first, then the quarterback. Against any other option, help on quarterback first, then play inside out on the pitch (Diagram #108).

  If key goes away, bounce in place while checking for a counter. If there is no counter and play is a running play, you must drive into the offensive center area first looking for bend back plays, then pursue from inside out. This is most important on a split 6 defense (Diagram #109).

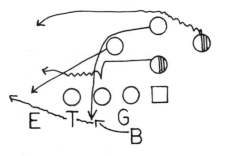

Diagram 108.

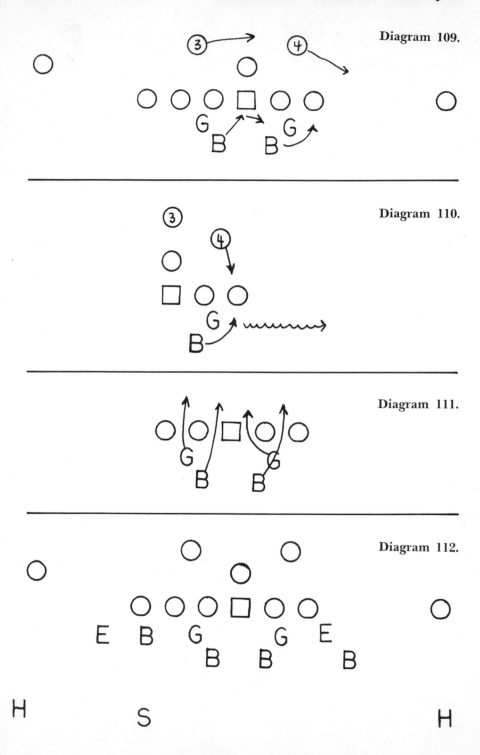

Diagram 109.

Diagram 110.

Diagram 111.

Diagram 112.

Weak Linebacker

A. DECLARE

Use declaring rules as set forth earlier.

B. STANCE AND ALIGNMENT

Same as strong linebacker.

C. KEY

Key #4.

D. PLAY AT SNAP

If #4 comes straight ahead or to your outside, fill the hole outside your guard first. If the point of attack is wider keep shuffling out parallel with #4 while determining run or pass. If it is a run, keep leverage on the ball (Diagram #110).

Backside option and flow away are played the same as the strong linebacker.

Blitz Rules

Both linebackers either fire straight ahead or cross charge with their guards (Diagram #111).

Pass Rules

All pass and motion rules the same as on the 6-2 defense.

44 LINEBACKER RESPONSIBILITIES AND TECHNIQUES

I've saved this one for last because 4-4 linebackers are a combination of all the other defensive schemes that we have already covered. There are a number of ways to get into a 4-4. First, there is the 4-4 popularized by Notre Dame. It calls for the strong linebacker to use eagle techniques, the two middle linebackers to use split 6 techniques and the weak linebacker to use the Will techniques of the 4-3 (Diagram #112).

If 4-3 is your scheme, there are two ways to get into a 4-4. One is simply to declare the strong safety weak and drop Sam back. Move Mike and Will over and you have a 4-4 (Diagram #113).

This is not quite as desirable because it involves some new learning. The easier way is to move Sam to the 60 linebacker posi-

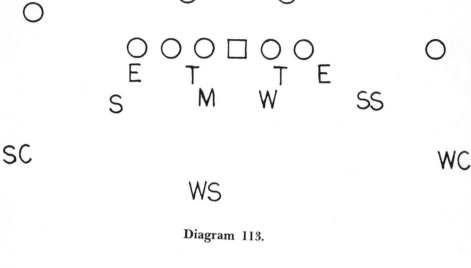

Diagram 113.

Diagram 114.

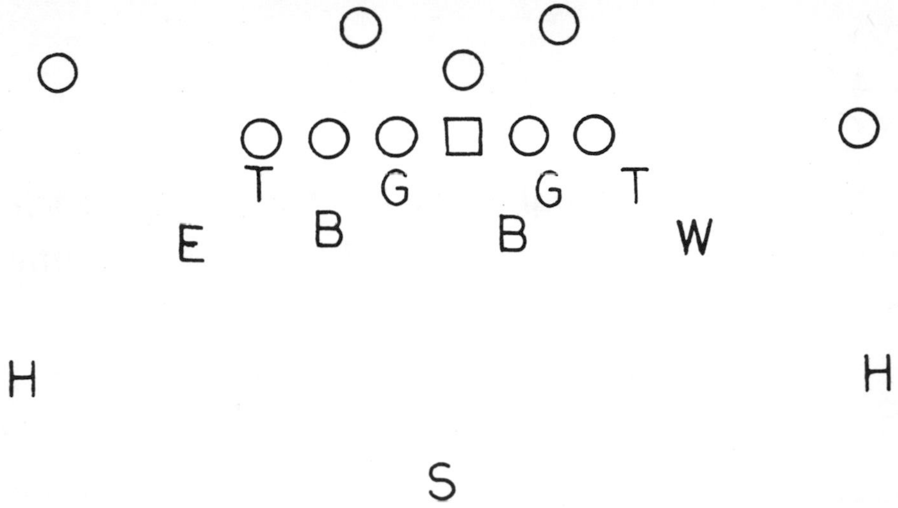

Diagram 115.

tion, Mike to the split 60 linebacker place and Will play is about the same as 4-3 (Diagram #114).

This scheme allows for the most carry over in teaching. Sam uses 60 techniques, Mike uses split 60 techniques, and Will uses 4-3 techniques. There is no big change for the strong safety. Considerable time must be spent with the strong defensive end. For that reason, it is advisable to flip-flop the strong and weak ends so that they learn tight-end and open techniques only.

There is one other way to get a 4-4 and that is from the 6-2 front. The ends drop off and now take the techniques and responsibilities of the strong safety and Will linebacker (Diagram #115).

This covers about all known schemes in which linebackers can participate. There is a great deal of overlapping in this Chapter and there are other ways to build a defense that could call for other assignments but by following one general theme of secondary coverage it has been possible to go over the basic differences in linebacker play association with the known popular defenses used today. As far as the 4-3 goes, the whole picture is explained in Chapters 7 and 8.

4

Toughening the Mental Approach to the Defensive Game

TRAINING THE DEFENSIVE SIGNAL CALLER

This is an area that has changed greatly in the last decade. It used to be that you worked long hours with your defensive quarterback and lived or died with his ability. I can remember many sessions with the signal callers going over flash cards or playing a game with little toy players on a small gridiron. It took so much time that the student-athlete simply could not meet enough to get the job done. He had regular practice and film study that all the players had, and his school work, and he just didn't have time to spend on learning to *call* signals.

About this time, side-line phones came into extensive use. The defensive chief was on the side line running the defense and hooked up with a head set to another assistant in the press box. This developed because of the poor vision on ground level. In order for the coach in the press box to do a good job of pinpointing the defensive breakdown it was almost mandatory that he know the defense called before the offensive play was run. The logical result was for the defensive chief to call defenses from the sideline. Now this worked well. A system of arm and hand signals could easily be worked out and thus relieve the player on the field and help the coach in the press box.

There was only one hitch. Opponents began picking up the signals. Finally we had to have a signal which meant "you call this defense." So now we had to go back and train them again; not as completely as before, but train them none the less. We also gave our signal caller the right to "wipe us off" any time he felt he had a reason for another call.

Without considerations for game plans here are some rules of thumb that we used:

1st and 10	Use your base defense mostly, blitz sparingly. Try to get 2nd and 7 or better. Stunt sparingly.
2nd and short	Use tough run defense. "Come to see them." Use stunts.
2nd & one or two	Use prevent defense. Make sure your deep people are deep. Let them have the first but no score.
3rd and long	Mix your best pass defense with the blitz. Don't blitz more than one out of three 3rd and longs unless it's going real good. Don't blitz on 3rd and long if you blitzed on 2nd and long.
3rd and short	The best you have to stop the run. Don't be afraid to mix the goal line defense in here. Get the secondary close.

There are many factors that could change this. The biggest is "What do they do best" or "What kind of team are they?" Another is "What have they been hurting you with?" Of course, time left in the half, or game, is important when considered with the score at the time. This can be affected by number of time outs your opponent has remaining.

Here are some examples: You have a narrow lead and there are two minutes left in the game. Your opponent is deep in his own territory and a field goal or touchdown will win it for him. If he has all his time-outs left, your double cover short people should play slightly inside the wide receivers. If your opponent is short of time-outs, then your double cover men should play outside the wide receivers to take away side line completions. Don't be afraid to mix in a blitz with deep zone coverage. If the time remaining is a minute or less, and your opponent has a good way to go, you should try to prevent his wide receivers from getting deep. A good plan is to put in another defensive back for a lineman and play a 3-8 ratio. This allows you to play the five eligibles man for man with a three-deep zone. Another thing to think about is replacing those three rushers with fresh players. This is especially true if your opponent has been throwing a lot in the game. Nothing can tire your defensive line out like repeated pass rushing. Very often three fresh rush men, against weary blockers, can get to the passer.

Here are some general hints that all defensive signal callers should have stuck up in their locker:

1. Be a leader (take charge).
2. Know everyone's assignments.
3. Always check the yard markers and the down and distance markers.
4. Anticipate your opponents sets but be prepared to check off.
5. Find out, off the field, what problems your teammates may be having.
6. Know your own personnel.
7. Know your opponents capabilities.
8. Keep hollering warnings of draw, screen and reverse. Sometimes you can talk a quarterback out of a call.
9. Have a reason for a defensive call.
10. Be the guy with the most pride in your defense.

INSPIRATION AND THE PSYCHE UP PROCESS FOR THE DEFENSE

This is a broad field and a whole book could be written about this subject. I will attempt to hit some important points, but when you are dealing with morale, you are dealing with many and varied human emotions.

The first thing that comes to mind about morale, or the winning edge, is that *"You can't win unless you really believe you can."* There is something very mysterious about the power of the mind. We have all heard about the *power* of positive thinking. But what does that really mean? I have a theory called "The Positive Molecule." This started out as more or less a joke but the more I've thought about it, and talked about it, the more I've begun to believe there is something to it.

The way the Positive Molecule theory works is that first you assume the mind emits something like an electrical current. Sort of molecules coming out in waves. These molecules can exert a physical force on people, places, and things. This "force" can actually change or influence the things at which they are directed. For an example, let's take the analogy of a man playing craps. For years I've seen crap games in Army barracks and troop ships and there always seems to be one guy who "cleans" everybody else. There is always this one guy. He always wins. Why? If you were to watch him, you would see the acme of positive attitude. He *knows* he's going to win. It follows (by the Positive Molecule theory) that he emits these powerful little molecules that come in contact with the dice and make them roll up what he wants them to. It may seem imaginatively ridiculous, but how else can you explain it? Of course, the reverse is also true. There is an old bromide which says "scared money never wins." Those people who gamble fearing that they might lose—usually do. I've heard guys going into a race track say "I'm not really a gambler, I just set aside a certain amount I know I can afford to lose and enjoy myself." They surely must lose whatever their limit.

This theory goes into all fields of human endeavor. It also affects health, love, and well-being—the whole ball of wax. I've seen people con themselves into all sorts of diseases and ailments. Conversely, there are shrines where "miracle" cures have taken place. Crutches are thrown away and the blind can see again. We are getting into the religious area, you might say, and you are right. I think there is a strong connection between the mind and the soul. The evidence of a soul is said to be the ability to reason. I just happen to think that by the temperature, or degree of mental output, a person can influence those things around him.

Now, how does this apply to the game of football? I really don't know of a better way to account for the stunning upsets we see every football season. When a team can compose itself as a group, all emitting those positive molecules at one time and in one direction, against a team who, though superior in talent and ability, is merely going through the motions or doing a job; then you have all the ingredients for one big upset. I'll even go a step farther by saying that when this condition exists you actually feel the "vibrations." The sidelines and locker room are almost electric. You just know you are going to win, you can actually "feel" it.

The next question is, how do you achieve this state? This is not an easy question to answer except that I know it starts individually and somehow grows into a team thing. Most kids are looking for this "feeling" and they just can't quite find it. Sometimes one of the players will prove to be the catalyst that lights the fire. Sometimes the coach can do it—sometimes he can't. The classic example of the coach doing it would have to be Knute Rockne's pre-game talk of "winning one for the Gipper." There, of course, have been many inspirational messages from coach to team that have done the job. They all generally fall into just a few categories. Here are some guide lines.

1. Be sincere yourself—if you aren't fired up or don't believe what you are saying yourself, it will show through and be of no value.

2. The idea, theme, or message must be emotional in nature.

Usually war, love, hate, struggle, adversity, triumph in face of great odds, etc.

3. Personal charisma—some men just don't have it, but you never know unless you try. Some coaches just don't believe in all this so therefore won't even try.

4. A loud clear voice that varies in tone, pitch and intensity. A lot of great thoughts have been lost simply because they weren't heard.

5. Change of pace—it stands to reason that you can't do the same type thing every week. I guess the hardest thing to do is sense just what is needed at the right time. Don't forget silence. There is something very dramatic about a silent dressing room.

6. Never appeal to your players to win for reasons that are personal to you, their coach. Always they must win for *themselves* and what the personal satisfaction to *them* will be the rest of *their* lives.

7. Never panic at half time. Just like in golf, you have shot a poor first nine but now you are making the turn and it's a whole new ball game. Very often golf pros can shoot a 40 on the front side and come back with a 31 or 32. Change a few things and get those positive molecules flowing again.

8. Always start the "psyche-up" process the night before the game. The emotions must build up to a peak by game time. Concentration cannot be turned on or off like a light switch.

9. Everything must be positive. Never use words like "if" or "don't" or "maybe." Those molecules must be pure positive. Mistakes must not be even brought up. Correct in the positive way by telling the offender what he must do and that you *know* he will.

10. About every three years the written and signed Pledge will be effective. Don't scoff at this one. A lot of kids will whoop and holler with false sincerity but writing maketh the exact man. Draw up a short paragraph or so that just bristles with enthusiasm and fight. Present it to the Captains the night before. Keep it secret. Have the Captains take it to the players and keep it after it has been signed. Never let the press in on this. I've got three of those stuck away in a drawer and every one of them were the hallmark of a great upset.

Well, I could go on and on, but what it all boils down to is that human response and human endeavor just aren't the same all the time. Like the degrees on a thermometer we put out measurable efforts and they are never the same. Coaches who believe that this phase of football will take care of itself are missing one of life's great phenomena. If it were up to these coaches, there would never have been a Horatius at the Bridge or a Sgt. York or a Finnish Army against the Russians prior to World War II. Great material and splendid organization will win most of your games but when you run into a small band of patriots who just won't be defeated—look out.

THE BUILD UP TO THE GAME

Setting the stage for the contest is as important as the contest itself. Our procedures here at the University of Florida may be open to some debate, but assuming we are playing a game on Saturday, here is what we did to build up to the game.

SUNDAY (6 days from game time)—Coaches grade and chart yesterday's game, and eat with the team Sunday night dinner. After dinner coaches and players split into respective groups and go over yesterday's game films. This should be "happy time." Find the good things and the funny things. Players should look forward to reviewing the game films. Personal mistakes and sharp criticism should be done with the coach and offending player privately. After the review, the players are excused to study and the coaches work on next weeks scout report and game plan. This is the coaches' long day—seldom will they be finished before midnight.

MONDAY—Coaches still working on game plan and personnel changes. Players come by in small groups to watch opponents films. Practice Monday is a light one without pads. The basic game plan is initiated. Coaches work again Monday night. Printed slogans, etc., are arranged for.

TUESDAY—By noon today written game plans must be turned into the Head Coach. After he reviews them and makes any changes, they are now printed for distribution. Practice today is work. Plan your work, work your plan. Breakdown drills are alive and all phases of the kicking game are covered. Sometimes coaches will be working Tuesday night if the game plan just isn't going right.

WEDNESDAY—Players continue on game films. Today all slogans, bumper stickers and like material is distributed. We have had a small plane fly over our practice and drop appropriate slips of paper on our kids during the practice. Practice today is polish and goal line scrimmage. Coaches call their high school prospects tonight.

THURSDAY—Fun day—Our practice is light and consists of review of all game plans. We allowed considerable horse play on this day. Linemen wear backfield numbers and vice versa, or maybe some players would sticker their helmets with the week's slogan—anything to relax the tension.

FRIDAY—We always had a long meeting with films today. Sometimes we would go to the field and walk through our assignments, but there is no organized practice. At 5:00 P.M. we arrange for the greatest meal possible. We really did it up nice. We had candle lights, stereo music, great food, everything we could think of to make it a "winner's meal." At 7:00 P.M. everyone meets in the projection room with a light bag packed prepared to spend the night at a motel outside of town. At this point the players' emotions are lying just under their skins. They really are searching for something to set the stage. Sometimes they lock the coach out of their meeting. Sometimes they ask for a special talk. Sometimes the staff has a printed letter or message. Whatever it is, it must happen now. The chill bumps have to rise and the adrenalin must start pumping. Then we show them a very carefully selected movie that has been rented in advance. This movie must advance the feeling of preparation for combat. There must be a maximum of action and a minimum of mish-mash. After the movie, the silent time starts. Only necessary conversation takes place. This is concentrating time. The bus ride to the motel is quiet. Upon arrival at the motel a hamburger snack is set up buffet style and the players eat what they want.

SATURDAY—Players sleep in until the pre-game meal at 9:30 A.M. After the pre-game meal, which is also buffet style, the taping begins on a schedule. The buses leave for the stadium at noon, arriving about 12:30 P.M. From 12:30 until 1:40 the squad dresses and finishes taping. At 1:40 P.M. warm ups begin and last only about 20 minutes. Then it's back to the dressing room where the final stage of the emotional build-up is laid out. Five minutes before game time the captains and coaches leave the squad and they have a couple of minutes to themselves. Lastly there is the coin toss, the Lord's Prayer and the kick-off.

5

Utilizing the Post-Game Study to Improve the Linebackers

HOW TO USE FILMS AND GRADING

With all the great techniques of motion pictures, TV, instant replay and the rest, we still don't have a good method of filming a football game. Good for grading that is. The secondary coach and the wide receiver coach want wide angle pictures so that all their players can be seen throughout the play. This reduces the size of the interior linemen to an extent where their techniques of play are hard to see and evaluate. If your camera man zooms in on the line, then the wide people aren't in the picture at all. The only obvious answer is to use two cameras. This is expensive and not everyone can do it. It also makes trade film packages too bulky to include both wide angle and close up. We found one alternative. TV films are mostly close up, so we graded every play from the wide angle as best we could. Then, we also used an extra TV film to go over stance and techniques for the interior linemen.

Grading and evaluation is almost a never-ending proposition. There just never is a point where you have done all there is to do. It is up to the grader and how much time he can afford. I've seen grading systems that are more thorough than mine, and I liked them, but Sunday just has so many hours and I found I could only handle six hours on player grading, scouting my own defense, and bringing the incentive charts up to date. This left me with two hours with the players and about four hours on next week's opponent. This, along with a couple of hours for eating and an occasional break, and I've already put in a 14 hour day. And we could never start before 10 or 11 A.M. because the films weren't ready. So from

101

11 A.M. Sunday morning until 1 A.M. Monday morning was about all the time there was.

Player grading boils down to a very few things that must be recorded. We figured that a player did what he was supposed to do, or he didn't. This meant we could grade him on a particular play either + or 0. Now the 0's can be one of three kinds. The player either loafed, made a mistake in assignment, or didn't use the right technique. So for every 0 we added the appropriate initial as 0L, 0M, or 0T. Also we added words for big plays and tackles made. A player's final evaluation would be a percentage grade such as— 40 plays, 10 zeros = 75% 7 tackles, 2 batted passes, 2 pass rushes, 2 blocks on a punt return. Let me explain why we didn't keep assists. This is a fine line that defies accuracy. If a player was a factor in putting the ball carrier down, we gave him a tackle, even if we gave three tackles on one play.

We never made a player's grade public, or for that matter, we never even let the rest of the team know each other's percentages. Each boy got his own grade privately. The reason for this is that we admit the human error in grading. No two coaches grade alike, and no coach is ever completely 100% objective. I know a lot of coaches use grades to establish their starters, and I just happen to think that this method *can* be unfair. Also there are other factors involved. Let's say you have a good sophomore pushing a good senior. They both play about the same. The sophomore out-grades the senior by one or two percentage points. If you start the sophomore next week the senior will get his nose out of joint and won't "push" the sophomore. As long as they are equal the sophomore will keep pushing the starting senior. There are some other factors, such as experience, clutch performance, etc. The fact is, the players themselves know who the starters should be. You can't fool them with slanted grades or anything else. Only a few times in twenty years have I ever had a dispute about starters.

You may say then, "Why grade?" Well, there aren't too many good reasons for it, but one very important one is that every play, of every player, should be watched in the films, and charting is a good way to make sure that you do it.

Just as important as game films is the use of practice films. It is shocking how many things you missed during a practice. You were right there watching every play and coaching your heart out. You came in from practice exhausted. The next morning you look at films of that practice, and you'll find that you missed about one half of the mistakes. This is particularly true of the secondary. We filmed all our perimeter drills, during the season, on Tuesday and Wednesday, and sometimes on Thursday. Films are the greatest teaching aid in coaching.

ESTABLISHING INCENTIVES FOR LINEBACKERS

This follows film use very closely. I mentioned earlier in this chapter about recording tackles, big plays, and other positive measurables. In our defensive film room we had a bulletin board with titles across the top. Under each title we had a list of names, in order, with a frequency number alongside. For instance, under tackles, the top name would be, say Jones 25. This meant that through this game, Jones had made 25 tackles. Each week this list was upgraded and the order changed. The next column would be fumble recoveries, then forced fumbles, then interceptions, batted passes, and block on punt returns. We had one more list called Hit Parade. This list was comprised of players who really hit somebody. It had to be a real head snapper . . . One that brings the "ohs" to the viewer. We let the players themselves vote on this list, and they were pretty circumspect. They rarely gave out more, than 7 or 8 a season. To summarize then, our incentive board was just a list of names under appropriate sections. It was a private thing and everything on it was completely measurable—except the Hit Parade and that was voted on.

There are always some people who want to recognize the player of the week. Sometimes a free hair cut or steak dinner goes with this honor. We tried to be honest, but always saw to it that all eleven starters got the goodies once. Before the season, we let our players know this and why. The reason is that we believe in team play and team spirit. Nothing is more important than the team. Our big, so called, star got one eleventh of the recognition from the coaches. After the season, all star selections will, of course, just pick one or two of your players. But at least while we were coaching them, they were all alike.

EFFECTIVE CONFERENCES WITH THE COACH AND TEAMMATES

One of the big problems in human relationship is lack of communications. This is the reason for all the so called "gaps." In order to prevent a "gap" between my players and myself, I often had informal meetings with them. I don't mean meetings when I sent for them, but meetings that just seem to happen. Whenever I had bed check or dorm inspection, I always would stop and just "shoot the breeze" with my players. Sometimes I just hung around the dorm halls or dining room in order to talk with a few players. During these meetings, rarely did we ever get down to the nitty gritty, but established a rapport that, at a later time, would enable a player with a problem to feel like he could communicate with me. After a while, the word spreads, and you, as the coach, have established the fact that you are willing to help. You are now communicating. It is surprising how many ways you can help your boys through the tough years of maturity.

Their problems always fall into just a few categories. Grades, girls, finances, small scrapes with the rules or laws, their place on the team, and their future are the most common causes of depressions. Since these things affect their playing ability, it is your job to eliminate the negative and accentuate the positive.

For those few young men who just won't "give" of themselves to a coach, their relationship to their teammates is most important. That is why it is so necessary that you as their coach have a rapport with *most* of the players. If you can get most of them going in the right direction, the rest will usually go along with their peer group.

Occasionally, a good athlete will come along who is a real loner. He has set up defense mechanisms against his coaches and teammates and almost defies the melting process of "fitting in." He is the hardest one of all to sell the importance of oneness to. Basically, he is not a team man because he is too wrapped up in self-consciousness to share. You can extend the hand of friendship over and over again, but seldom does it work. The only success I've had in dealing with this individual has been through the testing fire of the actual game of football itself. By this I mean that, prior to a big game, I have given this individual a wrinkle, or style of play, that was sure to spring him into a big play. Then I told him that if he followed the plan to the letter he would make player of the week, or all conference, or some high honor. Then, and this is necessary, he performed and whatever prediction I made came true. Of course, they don't always come true, but when they have, I finally won over the loner.

Conferences with the chronic discipline violator are the toughest for most coaches. This guy is almost a congenital misbehaver. He is in trouble all the time. And the funny thing about him is that he seldom will take the blame for his own indiscretions. Like the alcoholic, he can't be cured until he admits he is wrong. Believe me, they can think of many things besides admitting they are wrong. Unfortunately, most coaches have too many responsibilities to put up with this guy, and simply get rid of him after he has had several chances. Personally, I never felt like you saved anybody by firing them. I realize that you will lose all discipline if you don't dispense justice equally. I am for some drastic measures after the third or fourth offense. Somehow getting rid of this young man is just not the answer. Suspensions, withdrawal of privileges, extra running are all other methods. Another method of discipline is asking the offender to get up in front of his teammates and make a public apology. For some reason this embarrassment is much tougher on the sinner than anything else. Another way of chastisement is to have the player face a panel of coaches. There is something frightening about sitting in front of a semi-circle of men and having to face up to your mistakes in this air of judgment when you know you are wrong.

The last resort is dismissal. When that happens, we as coaches, have finally admitted that we have failed. In the ten years that I worked for Ray Graves at the University of Florida, we were only forced to do this a couple of times. It was always a source of pleasure to me that my boss had just about the same philosophy that I did.

The main reason for going into detail about rapport, communications, and discipline is that when one game is over and the next one approaches, you as coach must be able to have talks with your players individually about their play. If you haven't been able to talk with them about all these other things, you won't be able to talk with them about correcting their playing mistakes. The whole thing leads to the coaching conference. You must have a player's confidence. He must respect you. Not respect that you have demanded, but respect you have earned. Now when you coach him off of the field, he will believe you and try to improve.

A MODEL POST-SEASON STUDY

After every season, when recruiting had slackened and before spring practice, I always made a defensive report on the season. The main reason was to pinpoint breakdowns, but I'll admit to a little "horn blowing" when it was justified. Figure 5-1 is a verbatim copy of a report made on a recent season at the University of Florida.

DEFENSIVE REPORT

I. Our aim was to improve our rushing defense. This goal was accomplished. It is problematical as to whether we were that much better, or whether our opponents simply passed more because our offense put them behind early in every game. At any rate, we did improve from holding our opponents to 3+ yards per try to 2.2 yards per try in this season. Our opponents threw 59 more passes—so our pass defense yardage went up. There can be no conclusion drawn—except we got scored on too much. Eighteen TD's in 10 games is too much. Some TD's—there was no excuse for—just happened. *Examples:*

1965 :

2 vs Northwestern —Played 2nd Def. Unit too much
3 vs Miss. State   —Mistakes
1 vs LSU   —Was earned
1 vs NC State   —Was earned
4 vs Auburn   —Beat Deep Twice—Off. gave away two
1 vs Ga   —Was earned
2 vs Tulane   —Blk punt & Oskie set em up—2 caught out of bounds
2 vs Miami   —Pass int. & Punt hit Kirk
2 vs FSU   —Trammell mistake—contain 4th & 4, Grandy came up

It would seem 6 TD's were of a freakish nature (2 vs Miami, 2 vs Tulane and 2 vs Auburn). Still we were run over vs LSU and Miami some. Our goal line defense showed improvement. The 5-4 is not a good pass rush defense, still we threw our opponents for twice as many yards lost as they threw us. This report will show there was a definite "slacking off" defensively in the second half. Our opponents scored 29 points in the first half and 100 points in the second half. We got 5 less fumble recoveries and oskies this year compared to the year before.

STATS	AVG. PER GAME	RANK SEC	RANK NATIONALLY
Total Defense 2017	201.7	1st	7th
Points Opponents Scored 129	12.9	4th	
Rush Defense 884	88.4	1st	8th
Pass Defense 1133	113.3	3rd	

Figure 5–1.

% Completions

209Att/99 Comp	47.0	5th
Interceptions 15	1.5	4th
Fum Recoverage 13	1.3	4th
Punt Returns 394	39.4	Not recorded
KO Coverage 32/633	19.8 per try	"

II. In figuring plays that hurt—a system of down and distance was used—4 yds or more for 1st and 10, and any gain on other downs that brought up a short yards situation. The following are Stats from our 10 game schedule

GAME BY RANK	GOOD PLAYS	BAD PLAYS	PER CENT OF GOOD PLAYS
1. Ole Miss	47	12	80%
2. Georgia	57	16	79%
3. Tulane	54	16	77%
4. Auburn	37	15	71%
5. F.S.U.	42	20	70%
6. Miss. St.	45	20	69%
7. N.C. State	42	19	69%
8. Northwestern	45	21	68%
9. Miami	43	28	60%
10. L.S.U.	38	30	54%

III. We are aware that our second half performance defensively was way below our first half. This may have been caused by the fact that our offense put us ahead in every game at half time and our opponents fought back—anyway, using the above formula of good play vs. bad plays, here are the results.

Second Half

1. Auburn—We were 21% worse
2. NC State—We were 20% worse
3. Northwestern—We were 20% worse
4. Miami—We were 10% worse
5. Georgia—We were 9% worse
6. FSU—We were 8% worse

Figure 5–1.

7. Ole Miss—We were 7% worse

8. Miss. State—We were 2% worse

9. Tulane—We were 3% better

10. LSU—We were 10% better

IV. How did we play according to Down and Distance?

	GOOD PLAYS	BAD PLAYS	PER CENT OF GOOD PLAYS
1st & 10	165	93	64%
2nd & Long	111	37	75%
2nd & Short	36	32	53%
3rd & Long	94	23	80%
3rd & Short	13	17	43%
4th & Long	8	5	61%
4th & Short	0	1	0%

IN ORDER

3rd Long—80%

2nd Long—75%

1st & 10—64%

4th & Long—61%

2nd & Short—53%

3rd & Short—43%

4th & Short— 0%

V. COVERAGES—To be completely objective the "Passes Not Thrown" should be included. The first chart shows PNT's figured in. The second contains just passes in the air.

$$\text{BLUE} = \left.\begin{array}{l} 41 \text{ Hurt} \\ 95 \text{ Didn't Hurt} \\ \underline{35 \text{ PNT}} \\ 171 \end{array}\right\} 76\% \text{ Good}$$

$$\text{ORANGE} = \left.\begin{array}{l} 26 \text{ Hurt} \\ 42 \text{ Didn't Hurt} \\ \underline{3 \text{ PNT}} \\ 71 \end{array}\right\} 63\% \text{ Good}$$

Figure 5–1 (*Continued*).

$$\text{BLACK} = \left. \begin{array}{l} 25 \text{ Hurt} \\ 15 \text{ Didn't Hurt} \\ \underline{19 \text{ PNT}} \\ 59 \end{array} \right\} 57\% \text{ Good}$$

PASSES IN THE AIR

Blue — 69% Good

Orange — 61% Good

Black — 37% Good

VI. FIELD POSITION RESULTS

90 Starts

2 Down Area	6 Field Goals	Odds on Opponents
Opp. Goal to their 35	62 Punts	Scoring
	7 Oskies	15 to 1
	5 Fum Recover	
	5 Time Ran Out	
	3 Held on 4th Down	

32 Starts

3 Down Area	5 TD's	Odds on Opponents
Opp. Goal to our 40	1 FG	Scoring
	8 Punts	$5\frac{1}{3}$ to 1
	7 Fum Recover	
	3 Oskies	
	1 Time Ran Out	
	7 Held 4th Down	

14 Starts

4th Down Area	5 TD's	Odds on Opponents
Our 40 to our goal	2 FG's	Scoring
	2 Punts	2 to 1
	0 Fum Recover	
	3 Oskies	
	0 Time Ran Out	
	2 Held on 4th Down	

Figure 5–1 (*Continued*).

VII. BREAKDOWNS BY POSITIONS

	TIMES	
No. Player at Fault	5	.018%
Safety	9	.036%
Middle Guard	16	.065%
Ends	36	.073% (Each)
HB's	42	.075% (Each)
Monster	25	.102%
Tackles	54	.110% (Each)
LB'ers	58	.118% (Each)

We had 197 plays that hurt—3 areas caused 30% of the breakdowns.

23 Contain Failure
23 Missed Tackles
15 Penalties

BY POSITION

	MISSED TACKLE	PENALTY	CONTAIN FAILURE	MISTAKES
Safety	2			2
MG	4	3		1
Ends	2	4	8	1
HB's	3	2		2
Monster	0	2	1	4
Tackles	6	2	11	2
LB'ers	6	2	3	2

VIII. TYPE PLAYS THAT HURT US

TYPE PLAY THAT HURT US		TYPE PATTERNS THAT HURT	
1. 70 Passes	— 22	Side Line	— 18
2. Lead Passes	— 17	Hook	— 7
3. QB Ran (Contain)	— 15	HB Up & Delay	— 5
4. Sprint Out Pass	— 13	Down Out & Down	— 4
5. Sweeps	— 12	End Across	— 4
6. Ctrs & Reverses	— 12	Flat	— 4
7. Penalties	— 12	Flood	— 2

Figure 5–1 (*Continued*).

8. 1 Off Tackle	— 11	Quickie	— 2
9. Pull Up Passes	— 10	Flare	— 2
10. Traps	— 7	Curl	— 2
11. Play Action Passes	— 6	Break	— 2
12. FB Bend Back	— 4		
13. Option	— 4		
14. Hand Off	— 4		
15. FB Off T	— 3		
16. Flips	— 3		
17. Belly Option	— 2		
18. Quickie Pass	— 2		
19. Wedge	— 2		
20. Draw	— 1		
21. Screen	— 1		
22. QB's	— 1		

IX. RESULTS ON EACH DEFENSE

FREQUENCY

1. Straight, Hairy Straight, Double, ½ & ½ = 371 Times
2. Rover, 6-1, Goal Line   = 135 ”
3. Eagle Fire   = 38 ”
4. Slant   = 36 ”
5. G Fire   = 24 ”
6. Gator & Special & Bullets   = 17 ”
7. Eagle Regular   = 11 ”
8. Stack   = 9 ”

DEFENSES BY GAIN PER TRY

1. Eagle Fire   13 Runs + 37
                    8 PNT − 58
                 17 Passes + 86
                 38 Times + 65 = 1.7 per try

2. Rover   103 Runs + 226
                   9 PNT − 117
                 23 Passes + 183
               135 Times + 292 = 2.1 per try

Figure 5–1 (*Continued*).

3. Slant

26 Runs	+	39
4 PNT	−	19
6 Passes	+	69

36 Times + 89 = 2.4 per try

4. G Fire

17 Runs	+	54
1 PNT	−	10
6 Passes	+	27

24 Times + 71 = 2.5 per try

5. Eagle Regular

10 Runs	+	35
6 PNT	+	0
1 Pass	+	0

11 Times + 35 = 3.1 per try

6. Straight

173 Runs	+	640
25 PNT	−	216
173 Passes	+	781

371 Times + 1205 = 3.2 per try

7. Gator & Spec

12 Runs	+	38
0 PNT	+	0
5 Passes	+	31

17 Times + 69 = 4.0 per try

8. Stack

8 Runs	+	35
0 PNT	+	0
1 Pass	+	9

9 Times + 44 = 4.4 per try

X. FINAL GRADES

	PLAYS	AVG. GRADE	TACKLES	FUMBLES	OSKIES
Bennett	626	91%	57	2	5
Anderson	423	90%	58	1	
Matthews	445	88%	37	3	
Trammell	565	87%	32	1	5
Grandy	641	87%	53	1	3
Manry	81	87%	7		
Kirk	594	86%	52	1	
Pursell	387	86%	62	1	
Seymour	10	85%	1		

Figure 5–1 (Continued).

Hungerbuhler	10	85%	1		
Barrett	264	84%	30	1	
Hoye	376	83%	35		
Card	334	83%	56	1	1
Jetter	149	82%	10		
Williams	47	82%	8		
McCall	295	81%	33		
Colson	456	81%	47		
Pippin	23	80%	1		
Gagner	510	79%	52		1
Gio	142	79%	16		
Splane	182	78%	11		
Heidt	184	78%	28		
Downs	5	75%	6		
Holt	10	70%	8		
Warner	111	68%	6		

Figure 5–1 (*Continued*).

Part II

THE PERIMETER DEFENSE

6

Identifying Offensive Sets for an Unassailable Perimeter Defense

For years we have looked for a simple method of identifying offensive sets and formations. In the past, we struggled along calling this vast multitude of formations by the same terminology that our own offense used. Invariably we faced some that our offense didn't use, so we had to make up terminology. At best we were using names and letters that took a whole sentence to identify. At times, some of us were calling the same set by different names.

Finally, we solved this terminology thing by using our own defensive code. We were primarily interested in where the eligible receivers were, where the strength was and all that other wordage was unnecessary. Using this as a guide line we found out all football formations (excluding a few odd ball sets) boil down into three basic groups. There are either two eligibles on each side of the center, or three on one side and one on the other, or three on one side and two on the other. Simply by numbering them we found everything to be either a 22 set, a 31 set, or a 32 set. Naturally, the first number is the strong side. It really doesn't matter if these people are winged, flankered or slotted as long as you start from the strong side. If you desire more clarity, you can add some descriptive words, but this method greatly simplifies teaching.

This code is for recognition purposes only. Assignments are based on zones, or the numbering of all the eligibles from strength across. Start with the widest eligible to the strong side and number him #1. The next eligible in is #2 and so on through #5.

Following will be some examples of set identification with the eligibles numbered.

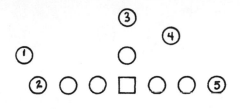

Diagram 116. 22 Set.

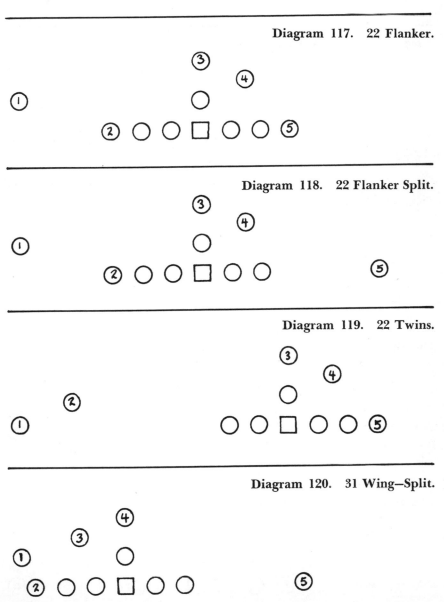

Diagram 117. 22 Flanker.

Diagram 118. 22 Flanker Split.

Diagram 119. 22 Twins.

Diagram 120. 31 Wing—Split.

Diagram 121.   31 Flanker.

Diagram 122.   31 Twins.

Diagram 123.   31 Trips.

Diagram 124.   32 Wing–Split.

Diagram 125.   32 Flanker Split.

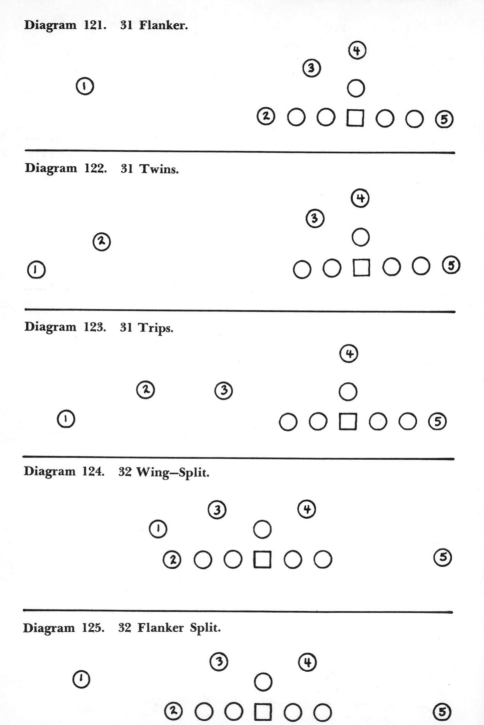

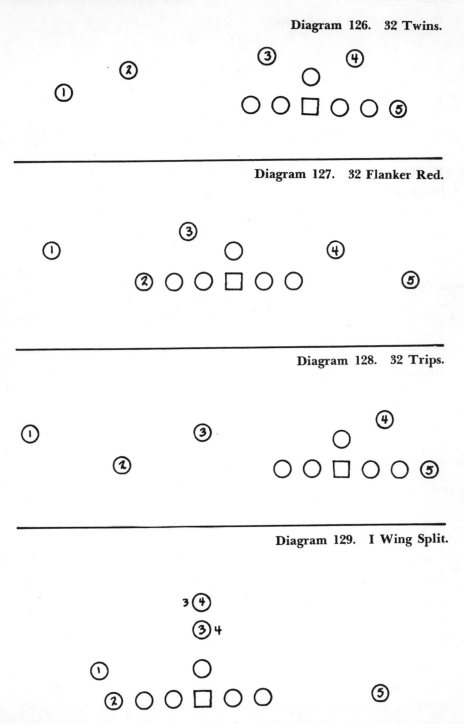

Diagram 126.   32 Twins.

Diagram 127.   32 Flanker Red.

Diagram 128.   32 Trips.

Diagram 129.   I Wing Split.

Diagram 130.   I Flanker Split.

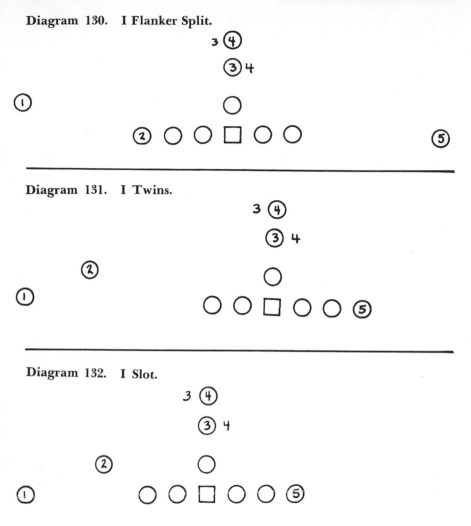

Diagram 131.   I Twins.

Diagram 132.   I Slot.

This was our identification system and method of numbering eligibles. The only other problem defensively as far as recognition and getting lined up correctly, is motion.

A SIMPLE METHOD FOR HANDLING ALL MOTIONS

Motion and fly motion have always caused defensive headaches. Here again we may be guilty of over-simplification, but we had to show our players that this motion thing was no big deal. To do that, we had to have a way of boiling all motions down to a few easy to recognize groups. The main thing is strength. Does the motion change strength or not?

We found out there was only one kind of motion that changed strength and that was nearly always a wing, slot or strong halfback going back to the other side. To do this he had to "cross" his backfield. So we called this "cross motion." There is also a motion away from strength, but does not change the strength. Such as a weak halfback going in motion weak. Since this was opposite from strength, we called it "counter motion." Any other kind of motion went toward strength and really didn't affect much, so we called that "strong motion." That's all there is. Cross motion, counter motion, and strong motion covers the whole field of motion. I did mention fly motion. This motion is too quick to do any adjusting so we just forgot it. It might affect an individual personal assignment, but it does not require a team adjustment.

Here are some examples of the three motions:

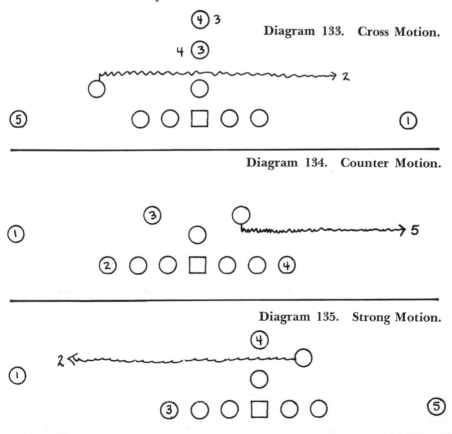

Diagram 133.   Cross Motion.

Diagram 134.   Counter Motion.

Diagram 135.   Strong Motion.

Now that we had only three things to worry about, we merely set up a few rules to cover these three eventualities.

The first thing that must be considered is, are you going to change your up front defenses because of any of these motions? Our answer was no, except where this was mandatory. For instance, if an opponent knew you would check out of blitzes on motion, they could keep you straight up all day.

Our system enabled us to play the defense called in every case except safety blitzes. We didn't safety blitz much, so I don't believe it ever came up that we had to check to a regular defense because our opponent ran a motion on us when we had a safety blitz called.

The best way to figure motion coverage is to align the offensive set up, assuming that the motion man aligned at that position right from the huddle. Then see how you would line up and cover that situation. From then on it's just a question of when their guy moves, our guys move.

Perhaps the best way to show you our rules would be to draw up the three motions against various coverages and blitzes.

First, we have called a reading defense up front and our basic coverage (Blue) which is a man coverage with a free safety. We get strong motion. See Diagram #136.

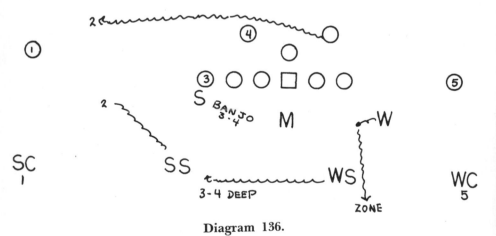

Diagram 136.

You will notice the motion has changed the numbers of the eligibles. Our strong safety and strong corner have #1 and #2. They can play them man or combo, depending on the communication call made by the strong safety. Sam and Mike play inside-outside on #3 and #4 (who were #2 and #3 so there is no change for them). Our weak safety comes over with the motion and takes our strong safety rules (#2 or #3 deep—in this case, it is #3 and #4). Will is now free and plays zone. On pass show he will back up into the area between our weak safety and weak corner, and look for #5 curling or running a post.

Next, we have called a reading defense with zone coverage and we get the same motion. If we have called a strong rotation, we have no problem. We just go ahead, execute a strong jump on snap and play it. If we called a weak rotation, we will have to change it by calling a strong jump. Our code word was "Jumbo Left." See Diagram #137.

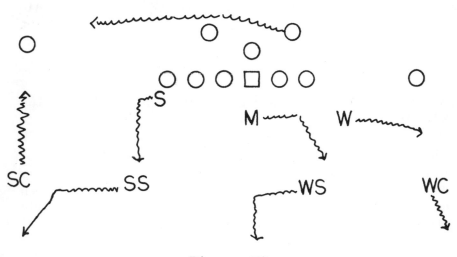

Diagram 137.

Again, we get strong motion and have a reading defense up front; however, we have called some other special coverage. We simply check our coverage back to Blue and play it as previously diagramed.

When we get strong motion and have called a blitz with Black coverage, we stay with the blitz and play man to man. The following example is Fire 1 vs. strong motion. See Diagram #138.

Notice that on Fire 1, Mike has called an "Over" to get himself in position to cover #3. The motion has changed him to #4 but Mike continues to stay on him man to man. Our strong safety takes #2 and our weak safety comes over with the motion and takes the strong safety's man. Everyone else executes a Fire 1.

Next we see strong motion again and have called a Fire 2, which

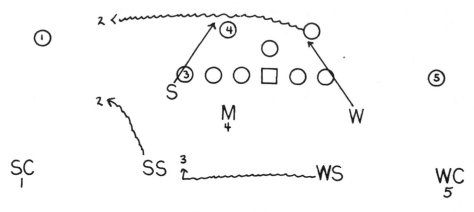

Diagram 138.

is a Mike-Will blitz. Everything stays the same except that Sam takes Mike's man. See Diagram #139.

We face the same strong motion but now have called a Fire 3, which is a Sam-Mike blitz. Everything again stays the same but our weak safety looks for either #3 or #4 to release, and covers whoever does. We don't think the offense can release both #3 and #4 when we blitz Sam and Mike strong and still protect their passer. Will plays zone since #4 went in motion strong. See Diagram #140.

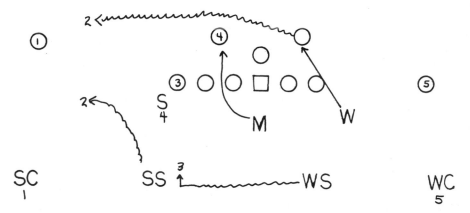

Diagram 139.

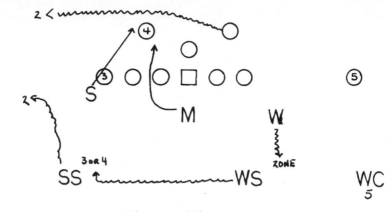

Diagram 140.

As I mentioned earlier, if we called a Fire 4 or 5 (safety blitzes) and we faced a strong motion, we would check out of it into a regular defense.

That covers strong motion against any defense we might have called.

Now, let's look at cross motion against anything we might call.

First, we go back to a reading defense with Blue coverage, and we get cross motion. What this motion always does, is to change strength. That means all our people designated as strong or weak must change to the opposite designation. Our weak corner becomes our strong corner, and our strong corner becomes our weak corner. Our weak safety becomes strong safety and the strong safety becomes weak safety. Sam becomes Will and Will becomes Sam. See Diagram #141.

Notice that Sam, who has become Will must back off the line and cover the tight end who has become #4 (Will's normal assignment). Mike rules stay the same.

We get cross motion and have called a reading defense with zone coverage. Again this is simply calling Jumbo Right or Left to the cross motion. See Diagram #142.

Next, we have called a special coverage and again we would check to Blue and cover cross motion as before.

We call Fire 1 with Black coverage and we get cross motion. This doesn't make any difference to Sam and Will because they are firing anyway. Mike would call an over to head up #3. Now #3 goes in motion weak. Mike must shift his tackles back the other way

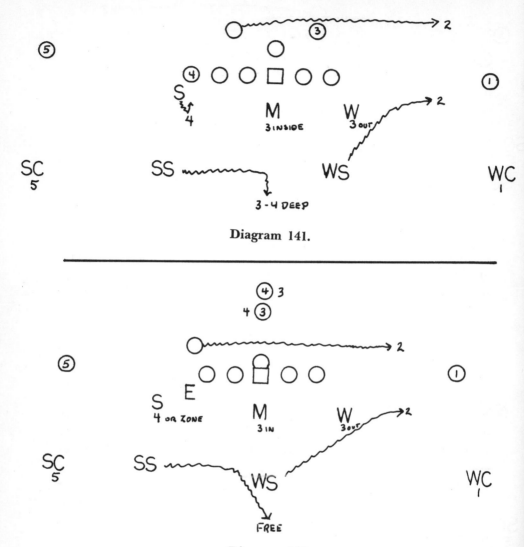

Diagram 141.

Diagram 142.

and get head up who is now #3. Our strong safety must remember that Sam is firing and therefore cannot cover #4 so he will have to stay home and cover him. Here again, it is extremely doubtful both #3 and #4 will release when we are firing Sam and Will. See Diagram #143.

We call Fire 2 with Black coverage, and we get cross motion. Let me add at this point, that while we expect Sam and Will to

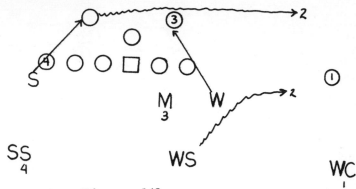

Diagram 143.

switch assignments on our reading defenses, when faced with cross motion, we did *not* ask them to switch blitz assignments. It created too much thinking for a linebacker getting cranked up to blitz. We put the thinking hat on our strong safety and asked him to know when Sam was firing and when he wasn't. Therefore, on Fire 2 Sam does not fire so he can cover #4. (He takes Will's assignments when not blitzing.) This means our strong safety must come over and cover #3. See Diagram #144.

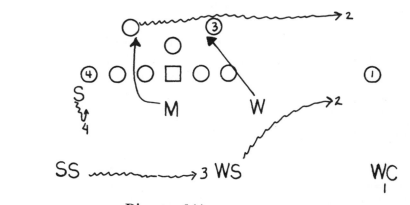

Diagram 144.

We call Fire 3 with Black coverage and get cross motion. This is not a good defense for this set, but rather than make any more exceptions, we just went ahead and played the defense called. Sam and Mike blitz. Our Strong Safety knows Sam is firing so he stays on #4. Will now is not firing so he has Sam's responsibility, #3. See Diagram #145.

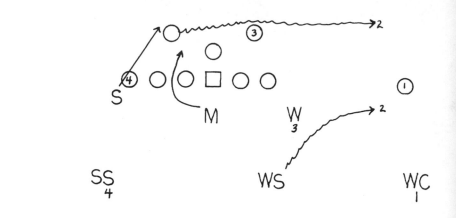

Diagram 145.

Again, if we had called Fires 4 or 5 (safety blitzes), we would check out of them.

This covers all our defenses against strong and cross motion. The last motion is counter motion.

I will go through all the defenses showing the moves, but this motion is pretty simple and only involves Will, the weak safety, and our weak corner. In general, Will covers this motion to a split end, and loosens off and covers the weak tight-end if the counter motion is to a tight-end.

We call a reading defense, Blue coverage. The motion man is #4. Will covers him unless there is a weak tight-end. Then Will must loosen up and cover the weak tight end who is now #4. In this case, our weak corner would have to expand and cover the motion man because he is now #5. See Diagrams #146 and #147.

We call a rotating zone either way and are faced with a counter motion. There is no need to change the direction of the rotation. Will must remember to go with the motion to a split end if the rotation is strong because he has weak flat anyway. If the rotation is weak, you are in good shape.

Counter motion against any reading defense and any coverage, except Black, is covered by the Will rules. Just remember, counter motion to a tight end is covered on any coverage, except Black, by

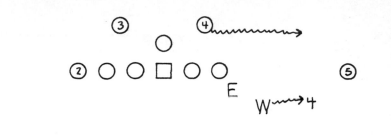

Diagram 146.

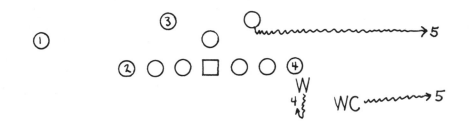

Diagram 147.

weak corner expansion and Will on #4 (tight weak end). Counter motion to a split end is covered by Will.

We call a Fire 1 or 2 and get counter motion (the two blitzes that include Will), our weak safety must take Will rules. Everyone else plays Black. See Diagrams #148 and #149.

If we face counter motion and have a Fire 3 called, there is no change. Everyone plays Fire 3. Since Will has #4, he plays it just like a reading defense and covers #4 to a split end, and the tight weak end if there is no split. See Diagram #150.

ADDITIONAL MOTION RULES

There are a few more motion rules. One situation I didn't mention, and that is a pre rotation, or prevent defense. In this set up

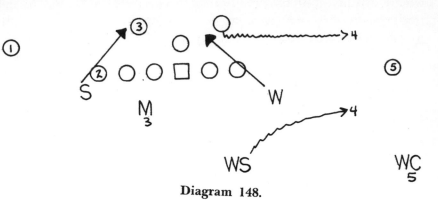

Diagram 148.

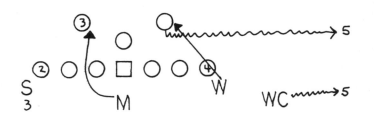

Diagram 149.

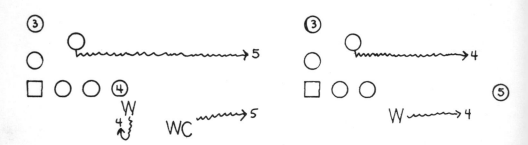

Diagram 150.

we are already double-covered on both sides, and any kind of motion, in any direction, is of no consequence. We are zone all the way and already lined up in it, so motion doesn't affect us. Also we have one other blitz—a Fire 8. This is a gambling defense which features eight rushers and three deep. If we call it, we go with it, knowing all the shorts will be open. If they can get if off, they have a sure gainer, as we aren't going to pay any attention to motion. Needless to say, we only call this one rarely. Also there is a different way to handle motion down on the goal line. This is covered in the chapters on goal line defense.

Before I finish with motion, let me add these few thoughts. Motion can become a bigger headache than it's worth. It isn't a red hot offensive weapon if you are sound and have everybody on your team in the right place. You could play all motions with one defense all day and do all right if your people are all lined up right when the ball is snapped. The only thing that makes you learn a bunch of extra rules is that you want to leave a blitz on, if you've called one. And the big reason for leaving them on is that offensive people can't run backs out of their backfield and still handle blitzes that might come from any side. This gives us the chance for a big defensive play, so we taught and learned all the preceding rules. Our opponents knew this and therefore didn't motion much.

7

Developing a Color Code System and Communications for the Perimeter

In Chapter 3 we covered linebacker responsibilities. To do this a portion of our coverages and terminology was used, so some of this chapter will be repetitive. However, this chapter will cover the whole perimeter, the pass defense, and run support, and we'll put it all together at this time.

Before we review the basic secondary defense, I'd like to explain why we use colors to name our coverages. The most important thing in coordinating coverages is communication between all members of the perimeter. Since they are spread out considerably more than the upfront people, voice communication is often impossible because of crowd noise. Therefore, we use colors to designate the coverage called. These colors are the ones that are a part of our uniform so that the coverage can be relayed by hand signal, simply by touching, or pointing to, the appropriate color. Also this makes signals from the bench a little easier.

First let's review the coverages that are applicable in this chapter.

1. BLUE COVERAGE

This is a coverage that can be zone, man, or a combination of the two, *but* always with a free safety. Simply, it is man for man for everyone but the free safety, *except* when two adjacent receivers align close together. When this happens we would rather play an inside-outside zone on just those two, close together receivers. The two defenders involved in covering these "close together eligibles" change from man coverage to inside-outside zone, and do so on a verbal call of "Combo," "Sambo," or "Banjo." The distance apart of the two eligibles is the factor in switching from man to zone. Six yards apart is our general rule. Bear in mind everyone else plays man; the "Combo" call would only affect the two defenders involved. Remember in an earlier chapter we explained that we number the eligibles from the strong side over, one through five. As an example, suppose #1 and #2 align as a tight end and close wing. Our corner and strong safety are responsible for #1 and #2. Since #1 and #2 are closer than six yards, our corner and strong safety would call "Combo" which means they will play an inside-outside zone on #1 and #2, instead of playing them man. See Diagram #151.

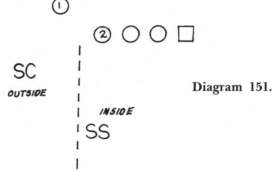

Diagram 151.

A Combo then is combination coverage between our corner and strong safety.

Suppose that #2 and #3 are close together. Our strong safety has #2, but knows that our Sam and Mike linebackers have #2 and #3 also. Since they can play these two eligibles reasonably well on all short to medium routes, our strong safety must help on either one who goes deep. In the case where both #2 and #3 end up going deep, we expect Sam to stay with the outside receiver deep, but also we should get some help from our free safety. The reason that we can get help from him is that both #3 and #4 can't get deep. If #3 is deep, our Will linebacker and weak corner should be able to handle #4 and #5 O.K. You will notice I said Sam had the "outside" of #2 or #3. Sam and Mike play a combination on #2 or #3 since they are most always close. This is called a "Banjo" or combination coverage with a linebacker or between two linebackers.

There is another call that affects the coverage of #2 and #3. It is called a "Sambo" and that means a combination coverage between the two safeties on #2 and #3. This is important because it is the way we can cover sprint outs and get containment out of Sam. When Sam hears "Sambo," he knows he is relieved of pass responsibility in the advent of a sprint out his way. Sam's rule is that both #3 and #4, and the ball, must come his way before he contains. If #4 goes weak, we cannot play a Sambo. Also the offensive formation can dictate a Sambo. Anytime #4 is behind the center, such as a strong set (31) or an I formation, we can call "Sambo" before the snap. When #3 and #4 both go strong *after* the snap, we play an automatic Sambo.

To continue with Blue coverage, Will always has #4 man to man. He could get help deep from the free safety, but we can't count on it all the time; therefore, he must always cushion #4 and anticipate a deep cut. Suppose now, that #4 and #5 are close together. This creates a "Combo" between the free safety and weak corner and thereby free Will who now plays zone or hook.

This is a capsule of Blue coverage. Later on in this chapter, I will go through the major formations and describe each call of all the coverages. In summary, here are the *basic* responsibilities on Blue coverage (Diagram #152).

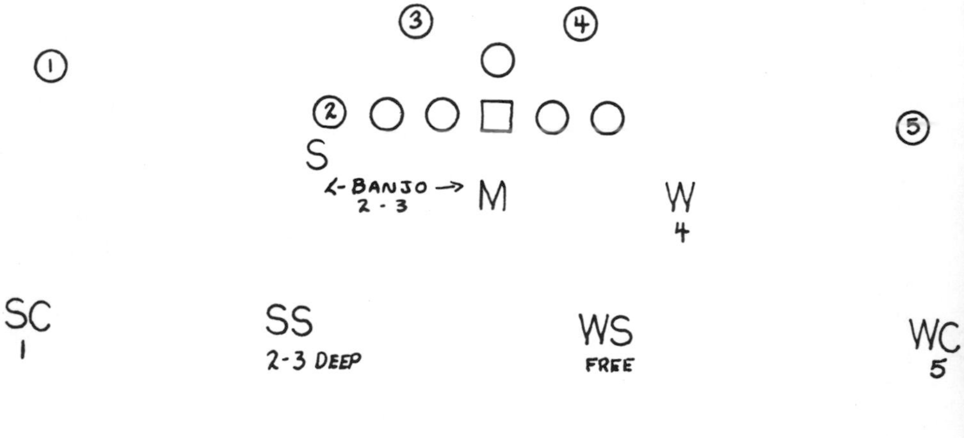

Diagram 152.

2. ORANGE COVERAGE

This is a zone defense all the way. It is our prevent defense and features a strong rotation with double cover on both sides. As soon as strength is established, our strong safety doubles on #1 and has the flat $\frac{1}{4}$ to his side. Sam has the next $\frac{1}{4}$ of the field up to 10 yards deep. Mike has the next $\frac{1}{4}$ over or the so-called weak hook area. Will goes out and doubles #5, if wide out, and has the last $\frac{1}{4}$ of the field up to 10 yards. Our corners have the deep outside $\frac{1}{3}$ of field, and our weak safety has the deep middle $\frac{1}{3}$ of the field. The short men, playing $\frac{1}{4}$'s, get position in the middle of their zone and play the ball, not the receivers. Let me add here that the Will linebacker and strong safety, who are in double cover positions, are coached to align either slightly inside or slightly outside the wideouts. They will take away one cut or the other depending on game plan, or time left, etc. They do this first and then get into their zone. There is one coaching point here. If #4 shifts up to a wide slot on the weak side, Mike will have to align in the middle of his zone prior to snap. Here again later in this chapter I will go through all sets versus this coverage but here is basic Orange coverage (Diagram #153).

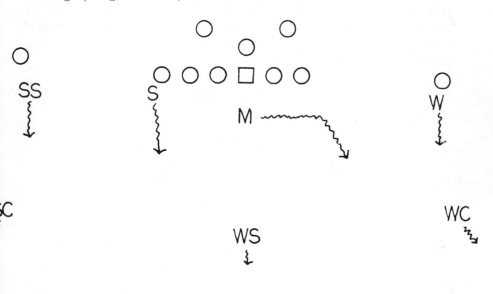

Diagram 153.

3. WHITE COVERAGE

This is an Orange coverage but only becomes Orange after the snap. It is a rotation on key. What it amounts to, basically, is an inversion between safeties and Orange rules for the linebackers. We didn't use this much, but on special occasions, where keys were infallible we got some use out of this type rotation. The first thing is to establish a key that will throw your secondary into a rotation where the strength is on every play. There is plenty of room for mistakes as the perimeter must all react the correct way on key. That is why I mentioned a clearly defined key is necessary. Suppose you play someone whose left half-back takes you to every point of attack and every pass pattern. He then is a logical key for rotation. You will always end up in a strong rotation towards your opponent's strength. There is another thing to think about before using this style of rotation. When your key goes weak, your weak safety becomes strong safety, and your strong safety becomes weak safety. This may not make any difference, but if you have selected players for these positions who are specialists, it may make a difference. Our weak safeties aren't usually as stout as our strong safeties, and our strong safeties aren't usually as fast as our weak safeties. However, as I mentioned, once in a while an opponent would come along whose offense was just right for this type rotation, and we would use it in that one game. Diagrams #154 and #155 describe a strong and weak rotation based on key.

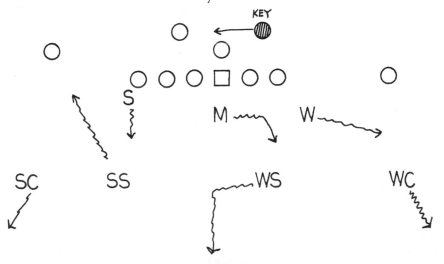

Diagram 154.

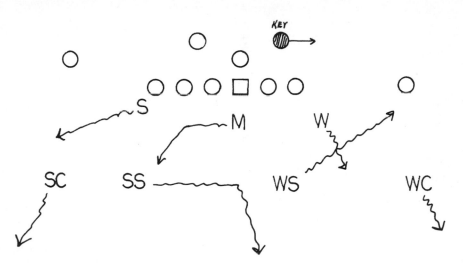

Diagram 155.

4. GRAY COVERAGE

This is one of those coverages that came along, due to a special need, that had no relationship to anything else. I don't know why we called it Gray—we just did, and that's the way we knew it. What happened was that we played a certain rival every year who featured the quick hitches and quick outs, and who pecked away at the short zones with regularity. They could throw the bomb also. We needed a coverage that would allow us to cover the five eligibles close and quick and still protect us from #1 or #5, or both, breaking deep for the bomb. By bringing our corners up just before snap we could play #1 and #5 very tight. We assigned #2 to Sam, #3 to Mike, and #4 to Will. This left us with two free safeties. Our strong safety could back up the strong corner and our weak safety could back up our weak corner. We were able to take away the quick passes to the wide outs and still protect ourselves deep. We just got to calling it Gray and here is a diagram of this coverage (Diagram #156).

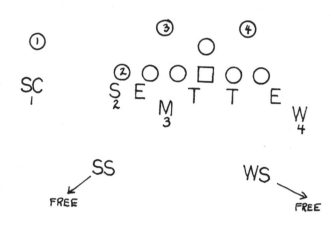

Diagram 156.

5. BLACK COVERAGE

This is the coverage we used on all blitzes. It is just man for man coverage, without a free safety. The reason we don't have a free safety is that when you blitz two of your three linebackers, you can still cover all five eligibles by using the remaining linebacker and the free safety. We rarely blitzed all three linebackers. When we did, it was against an opponent who never utilized all five receivers or was in a formation where he couldn't. Here, like in Blue coverage, when two adjacent receivers got close together, we used Combos, Sambos, and Banjos. When #1 and #2 eligibles are close, our strong corner and strong safety played Combo. When #2 and #3 eligibles were close our strong safety could play a Combo with Sam or Mike —which is a Banjo. Of course, if both Sam and Mike were blitzing, our strong safety would have to play a Sambo with the weak safety on #2 and #3 in close alignment. Again if #4 and #5 were close our weak safety and weak corner would play a Combo on them. The theory here is that our opponent should not be able to get receivers deep when we are blitzing two linebackers; therefore, we can operate without a free safety. As with the other coverages, I will go through most of the possible sets and indicate the proper rules. Diagram #157 is a basic Black coverage:

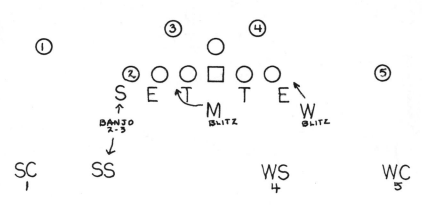

Diagram 157.

6. DOUBLES

Once in a while you will run across a hot receiver who aligns in the #1 spot, the #2 spot, or the #5 spot. The best way to always have double coverage on him, without playing zone all day, is to call doubles off of Blue coverage. It doesn't affect Sam or Mike—they just play Blue rules. It does affect Will when the hot receiver is in the #5 spot. Will doubles him short. When the object of the double is in the #1 position, our strong corner jumps him and plays him short while our strong safety plays him deep. Our weak safety comes over and takes the strong safety rules. Sam and Mike play Blue. Will has #4 Bakerman (term for "man all the way"), and our weak corner has #5. See Diagram #158.

When the dangerous man is in the #2, or slot, position, we will play him inside-outside with the two safeties. Our strong corner covers #1. Sam and Mike play Blue on #3. Coaching point: Sam walks off because our end can now stand up and contain. Will plays Bakerman on #4. Our weak safety has #5. See Diagram #159.

The hot receiver aligns in the #5 spot, and Will goes out and plays him short, and our weak corner plays him deep. Our weak safety now has #4 man. Sam and Mike play Blue. Our strong

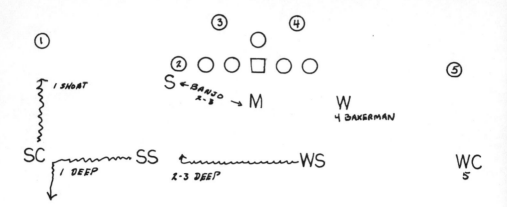

Diagram 158.

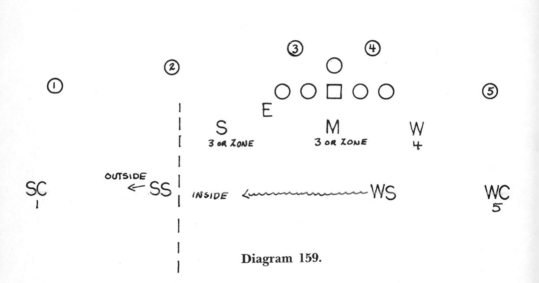

Diagram 159.

safety has #2 man and #1 is, of course, covered by our strong corner. See Diagram #160.

We have now covered this dangerous receiver short and deep when he is in the #1 or #5 positions, and inside-outside when he is in the #2 position. The calling of this coverage is simple. We call Blue-Double in the huddle. When our opponent breaks his huddle, we locate the receiver and call "one," "two" or "five."

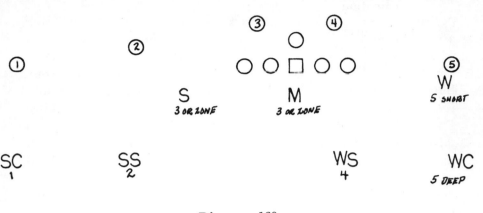

Diagram 160.

7. JUMP

This is Orange coverage pre-declared. The call in the huddle is "Strong Jump" or "Weak Jump." In the case, again, of the "hot receiver," we can call just "Jump" and wait until he lines up. Also we might have to change our jump because of motion or shift. Our word for this was "Jumbo." As an example, we have called Strong Jump. Our opponent comes out with their good receiver to the weak side or they use cross motion. We can change the jump by calling "Jumbo" and the direction. Diagram # 161 is an example of Jump coverage (which is Orange rules).

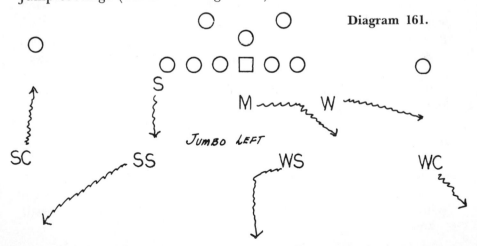

Diagram 161.

Blitz Coordination

I didn't go over this under Black coverage because it really isn't a coverage but merely a system of remembering who covers who when two of the three linebackers are blitzing. We used the term "Fire" for a blitz. We had three basic blitzes, or fires, which combine all combinations of two out of three linebackers going into rush the passer or play the run. They are Fire 1 (Sam and Will), Fire 2 (Mike and Will), and Fire 3 (Sam and Mike). We also had two safety blitzes, and one reckless defense named Fire 8 in which all three linebackers and the strong safety blitzed. If we only wanted one linebacker to go, we would add that backers name to the defense. Example, "43 Mike." If we wanted all three linebackers to go, we added the name of the remaining linebacker to the blitz calling for the other two to blitz. Example: "43 Fire 1 Mike." Where these linebackers blitz is covered in the next chapter, but it isn't hard to change blitzes from week to week, as long as the blitz involves the same positions. Here are a few simple rules for coordinating coverage with the blitzes.

1. When Will goes, the weak safety must take #4 man to man.
2. When Sam goes, the strong safety takes #2 and Mike takes #3.
3. When Mike goes, Sam takes #3 and the strong safety continues on #2.
4. When Sam and Mike go, Will takes #4 (Bakerman) and the safeties play a Sambo on #2 and #3.
5. When the weak safety goes, Will must play Bakerman (#4).
6. When the strong safety goes, our weak safety takes #2. Either Sam or Mike takes #3 (whoever is not blitzing) and Will plays Bakerman on #4.

As you can see this is just a matter of substituting. All positions will be covered in the next chapter.

Before we go through all coverages against major sets, let's review, in capsule form, the necessary terminology.

Blue Coverage. Man for man coverage on all five eligibles with one free Safety.

Orange Coverage. A pre-declared strong rotation with three deep zone, double covered on both sides.

White Coverage. Orange coverage arrived at after snap, on key. A safety invert.

Gray Coverage. Man to man coverage on all five eligibles with two free safeties.

Black Coverage. Man to man coverage on all five eligibles with six defenders blitzing.

Blue Doubles. A coverage that enables you to double-cover a great receiver if he aligns in either wide position or a slot.

Jump. A pre-declared rotation either way, or to an individual on the offense. Also a zone rotation that can be changed due to alignment or motion.

Combo. Inside-outside zone coverage between either Safety and their corner.

Sambo. Inside-outside zone coverage between Safeties.

Banjo. Inside-outside zone coverage between linebackers or between the Strong Safety and one linebacker.

Jumbo. Communication call to perimeter designating, or changing, zone rotation.

Number. When a member of our secondary calls the number of an offensive eligible, it means that he has him man for man.

Bakerman. Man coverage by Will on #4 with no free safety.

Red Set. Four eligibles who can get deep quick without harassment.

Triangle. QB and remaining backs in any set.

#1—Outside strong receiver.

#2—Second receiver from outside in, on the strong side.

#3—Third receiver from outside in, counting from strong side.

Most always the offensive fullback.

#4—Fourth receiver from outside in, counting from the strong side.

Most always the offensive running back or tail back.

#5—The widest receiver on the weak side.

22 Set. Two eligibles on each side of the center with a player in the normal fullback position.

31 Set. Three eligibles on one side of the center with one on the other side.

32 Set. Three eligibles on one side of center and two eligibles on the weak side.

Forceman. Defensive player responsible to play the wide run or take the pitch on options.

You. Call made by a Safety to his Corner telling him to be forceman.

Me. Call made by a Safety to his Corner telling him that he will be forceman.

Him. Call made by Strong Safety to Sam telling him to be forceman.

2nd Back Out. When remaining back of the triangle releases out after, and on same side, as the nearest back has released.

STRENGTH DECLARING RULES

1. Declare to an unbalanced line.
2. Declare to the flanker in a 22, 31, or 32 set.
3. Declare away from a split end.
4. Declare to the field on balanced 22 sets.
5. Declare to our left versus a balanced 22 set in the middle of the field.
6. Declare to the tight end on a Red Set.

BLUE COVERAGE VS. MAJOR FORMATIONS

1. 22 Tight (Diagram #162)

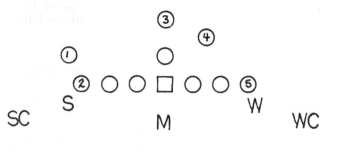

Diagram 162.

Sam	Align "O" position, 3 point stance. Flow to, use progressive keys E, G, or B. Contain sprint out. Flow straight back, shuffle out play Banjo on #2 or #3 with Mike. Flow away, harass TE and cover short across or pursue back of LOS.
Mike	Align normal. Key #3 on 43 inside, and center on 43 outside. Versus run use Mike techniques described in Chapter 3. Versus pass, play inside on #2 or #3. If #3 goes weak, stay with him. If #3 blocks, play zone to strong side. Draw and screen responsibility.

Will	Align in "H" position on tight end. Versus run use Will techniques in Chapter 3. Versus pass force #5 to outside and play zone because you know our WS and WC will play Combo on #4 and #5.
Strong Corner	Play Combo with Strong Safety. You are always the forceman on all Combos. Key #1 and #2; if *either,* or both, block on Sam, support (become forceman) right now.
Strong Safety	Play Combo with your Strong Corner. This is a "You" call. Key #1 and #2. If both block on Sam, support cautiously by filling straight up first, then be able to take either inside or outside run. If either #1 or #2 releases, cover him. You have running pass responsibility deep.
Weak Safety	Play Combo with your Weak Corner on #4 and #5. This is a "You" call and your responsibilities are the same as the Strong Safety's.
Weak Corner	Play Combo with Weak Safety. Your rules and techniques versus this set are the same as the Strong Corner's.

2. 22 Flanker Split (Diagram #163).

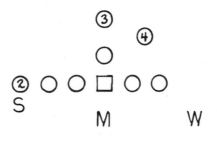

Diagram 163.

Sam	Align "H" position, two point stance. Use run keys set forth in Chapter 3. Versus pass, flow your way, contain. Flow straight back or pull up, shuffle out, play Banjo with Mike. If #3 blocks, and #2 is not in the flat, look up the curl or Post by #1.
Mike	Same as rules on 22 Tight.
Will	Align tight, regular, or walk off according to plan, field position, or defense called. Give your end a call of "in" or "out." Key #4. Against run use techniques in Chapter #3. Versus pass, cover #4 if he releases your side. Always play him for a possible deep cut. If #4 blocks or goes strong, shuffle back into area between your W.C. and W.S. and look for curl or post by #5.
Strong Corner	Align 8 yards off of #1, slightly outside of him but never get closer to sideline than 8 yards. Make number call to your Strong Safety and play #1 man. You will get a "me" call from your S.S. If #1 cracks back to the inside, holler "crack" and be ready to become forceman. This automatically changes the call from "me" to "you."
Strong Safety	Align even with your Strong Corner slightly outside of Sam. Call "me" to your S.C. Key #2. If he blocks, support outside of Sam. If you hear "crack," change to a "you" call and stay back, avoid crack block, but look for fake crack and run pass. If #2 releases inside and flow is away, shuffle over and become safety. You have #2 or #3 who might release deep, you do not have short across. If #2 and #3 release deep, stay with inside receiver until, or if, your WS releases you to help deep on the outside deep man. Be conscious of flow. If #4 comes strong, you know that your WS is coming over and that you are going to play an automatic Sambo on #2 and #3. You can now come up and cover the outside receiver in the flat. Sam will be containing.
Weak Safety	Align even with your S.C. and S.S. and over the offensive remaining HB (#4) unless he is in an I formation or 31 set. Then align over the offensive center. You will get a *number* call from your

Weak Corner. This makes you "free." Key #4. If he releases your side, back up and help Will and your Weak Corner on #4 and #5. If #4 blocks on pass show help to the strong side. If #4 sprints strong, play a Sambo with your S.S. If #4 blocks and weak run shows, support; this is a "Me" call.

Weak Corner   Everything is the same as the Strong Corner except you are keying and covering #5.

3. 31 "I" Slot (Diagram #164).

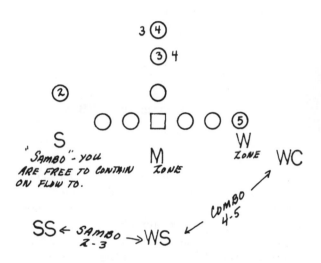

Diagram 164.

Sam   Since #1 and #2 are split out, you align head up #2 until he gets more than six yards out from the formation. Go to the walk off position as your end can now stand up and contain. If #2 is six yards or less, play him exactly as if he were the tight end and use the same keys and rules. If #2 is split out more than six yards, you know that your S.S. will play him either Combo with your S.C., Sambo with your W.S., or man. This now puts you into a Banjo with Mike on #3

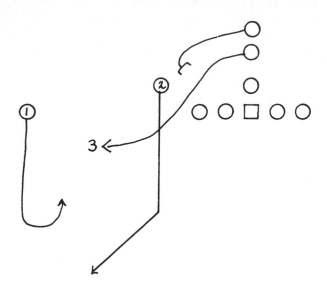

Diagram 165.   FB is #3.

	only. #3 is now your run key also. If #3 blocks on pass show, play zone.
Mike	Same as versus a 22 set except #2 may have removed himself.
Will	Same as versus a 22 set with a weak tight end.
Strong Corner	Work with Strong Safety. If #1 and #2 are close, play a Combo, if not, call a number and play man.
Strong Safety	Work with Strong Corner and Weak Safety. Depending on split of #1 and #2, you will either play Combo with your S.C. on #1 and #2, or if you get a number call from your S.C., you will play man on #2 giving a number call to your Weak Safety, or, if #2 and #3 are still close, you could play Sambo with your Weak Safety on #2 and #3. All other keys run or pass are the same as outlined versus a 22 flanker split.
Weak Safety	Align over center and communicate with your S.S. and W.C. You can now play *both* a Sambo with your S.S. and a Combo with your W.C. if the

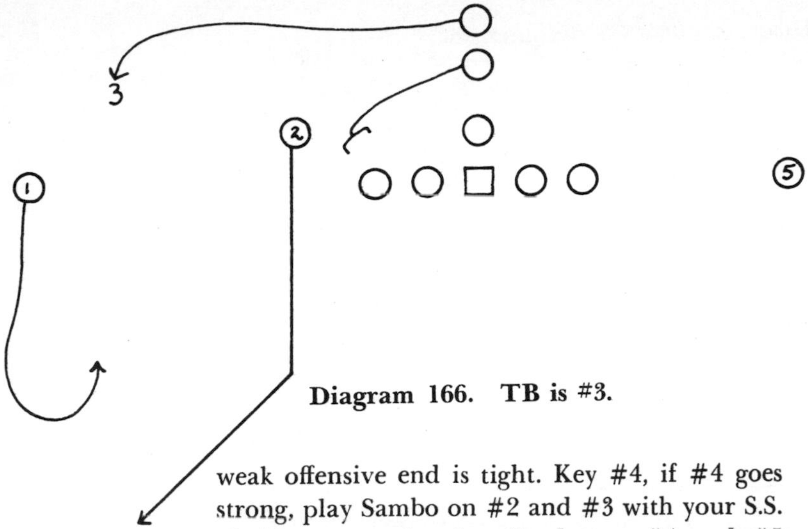

Diagram 166.   TB is #3.

weak offensive end is tight. Key #4, if #4 goes strong, play Sambo on #2 and #3 with your S.S. If #4 goes weak, play Combo on #4 and #5 with your W.C. If #5 is split, your weak side play is the same as outlined against a 22 set, you are free.

Weak Corner   Play Combo or Man depending on split of #5. Use 22 set rules.

Note   Anytime the offense is in an I formation, #3 and #4 can be either. The one that releases strong is #3 and the one that releases weak is #4. Also if they cross #3 becomes #4 and #4 becomes #3. See Diagrams #165 to #168.

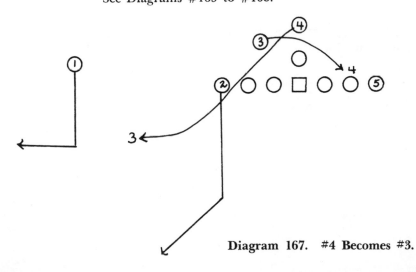

Diagram 167.   #4 Becomes #3.

Diagram 168.   #3 Becomes #4.

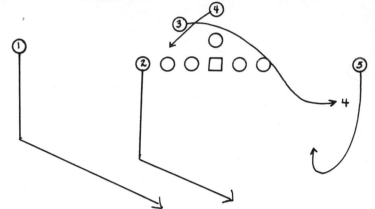

Diagram 169.

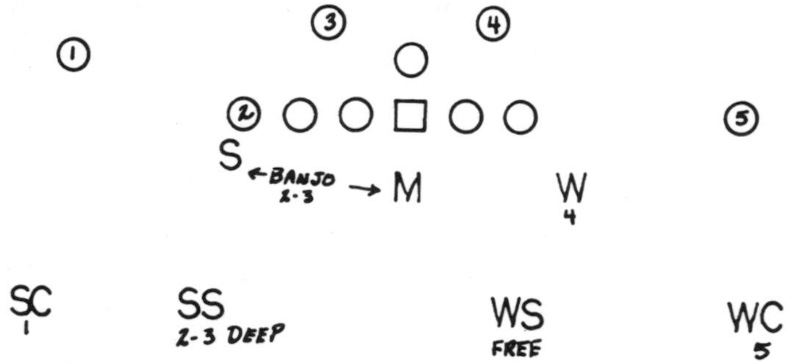

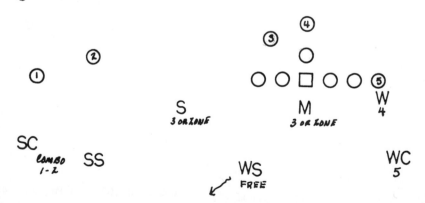

Diagram 170.

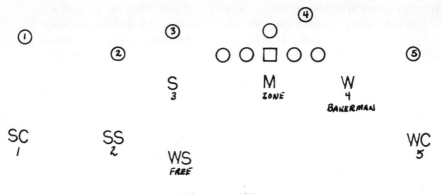

Diagram 171.

4. 32 Flanker Split (Diagram 169).

Sam	Same as versus a 22 Flanker Split.
Mike	Same as versus a 22 Flanker Split.
Will	Same as versus a 22 Flanker Split.
Four Deep	Same as versus a 22 Flanker Split.

5. 31 Strong Twins (Diagram 170).

Sam	Same as outlined versus 31 slot. If #3 blocks or option shows, become forceman.
Mike	Same as versus 22 set.
Will	Exception here. #1 and #2 are so wide away that your Weak Safety must favor that side and can't play Combo with your Weak Corner. This means you are back on #4 man. Your Strong Safety should give you a "Bakerman" call.
Strong Corner and Strong Safety	This is Blue, so play Combo on #1 and #2.
Weak Safety	Cheat over to head up #3. Key #4 but be in position to cover #1 or #2 on deep routes. Give "Bakerman" call to Will.
Weak Corner	Cover #5 man for man.

6. 32 Trips (Red Set) (Diagram 171).

Sam	Play #3 man.
Mike	Same as 22 Flanker Split.
Will	#4 Bakerman.

Strong Corner and Strong Safety   Play Combo or Man on #1 and #2.

Weak Safety   Split the difference between #3 and #4 on alignment. If #4 was in the fullback position, you can favor #3 a lot more. Also if #4 is in that position, you can help deep on #1, #2, or #3 right now; however, if #4 is slotted weak you will help on #4 and #3 deep. Give Will a "Bakerman Call."

ORANGE COVERAGE VS. MAJOR FORMATIONS

I have covered Orange and Jump rules previously so this is just a question of alignment. Diagrams #172 to #177 will cover Orange versus these major sets.

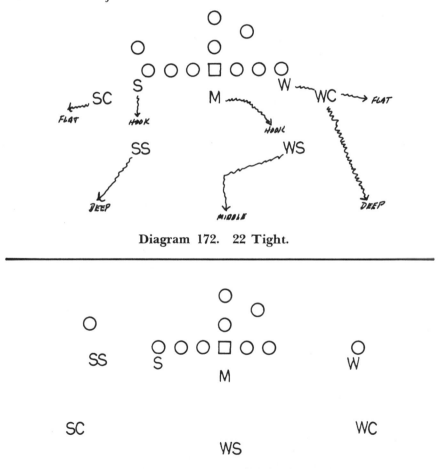

Diagram 172.   22 Tight.

Diagram 173.   22 Flanker Split.

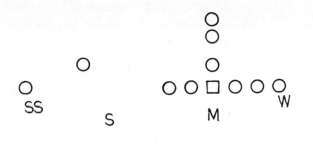

Diagram 174.   31 I Slot.

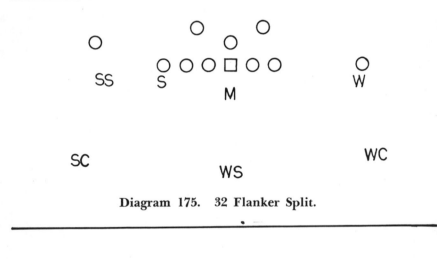

Diagram 175.   32 Flanker Split.

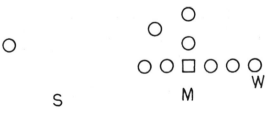

Diagram 176.   31 Strong Twins.

Diagram 177. 32 Trips.

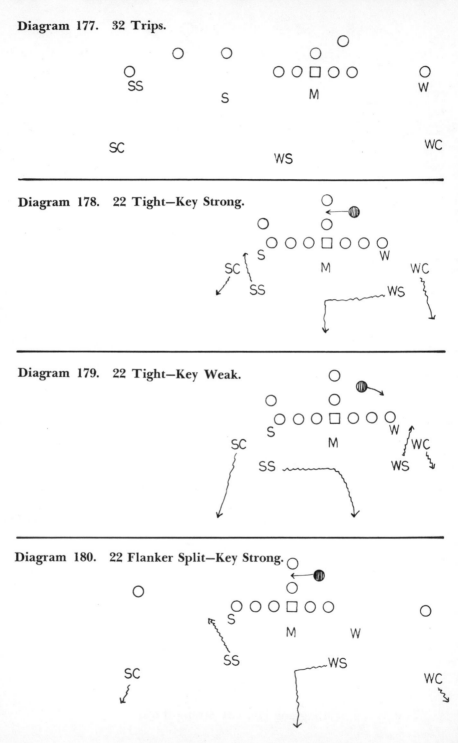

Diagram 178. 22 Tight—Key Strong.

Diagram 179. 22 Tight—Key Weak.

Diagram 180. 22 Flanker Split—Key Strong.

WHITE COVERAGE VERSUS MAJOR SETS

There are no changes from zone rules. Our corners are always going to play the deep outside ⅓'s. The safeties are always going to rotate on key. Linebackers are going to take zones away from the key on pass show. So, again, the best way to show this is by diagrams (Diagrams #178 to #186). For purposes of example, let's use the offensive left halfback as a Key.

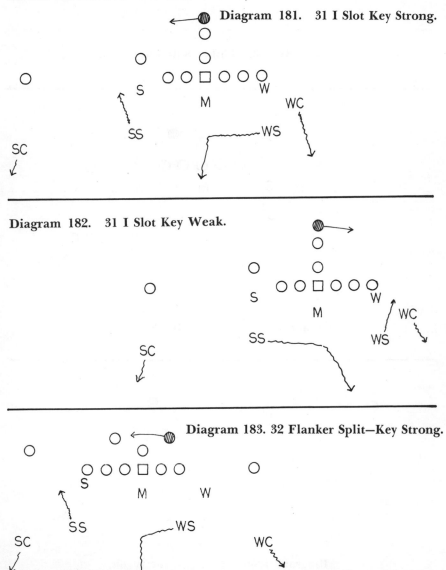

Diagram 181.   31 I Slot Key Strong.

Diagram 182.   31 I Slot Key Weak.

Diagram 183. 32 Flanker Split—Key Strong.

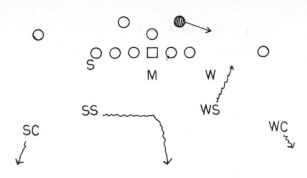

Diagram 184.   32 Flanker Split—Key Weak.

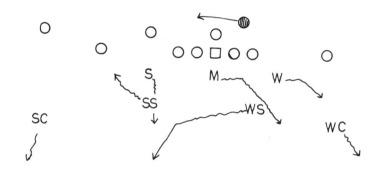

Diagram 185.   32 Trips—Key Strong.

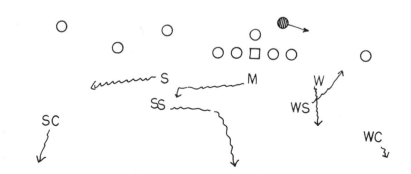

Diagram 186.   32 Trips—Key Weak.

GRAY COVERAGE VERSUS MAJOR SETS

Gray, as I mentioned earlier, is a special coverage that is geared to people who play wide receivers. There is no point in attempting it against tight sets. See Diagrams #187 to #191.

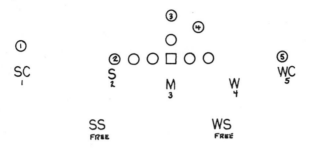

Diagram 187.   22 Flanker Split.

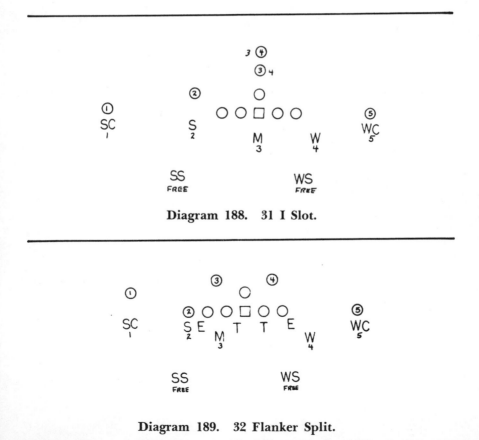

Diagram 188.   31 I Slot.

Diagram 189.   32 Flanker Split.

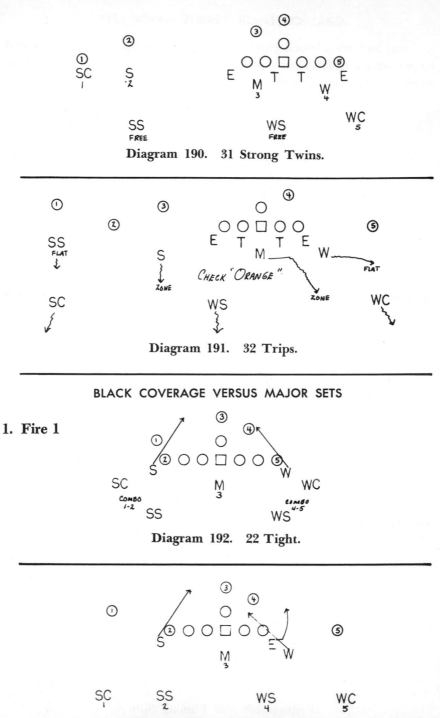

Diagram 190.   31 Strong Twins.

Diagram 191.   32 Trips.

BLACK COVERAGE VERSUS MAJOR SETS

1. Fire 1

Diagram 192.   22 Tight.

Diagram 193.   22 Flanker Split.

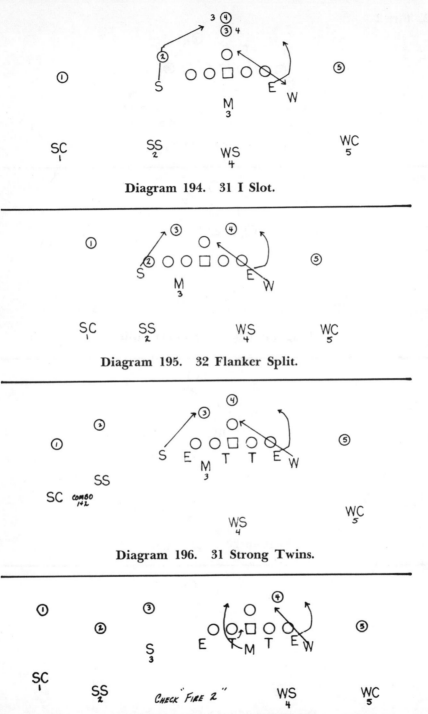

Diagram 194.   31 I Slot.

Diagram 195.   32 Flanker Split.

Diagram 196.   31 Strong Twins.

Diagram 197.   32 Trips.

2. Fire 2

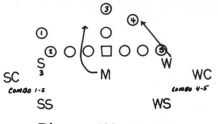

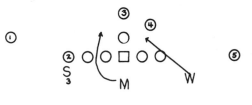

Diagram 198. 22 Tight.

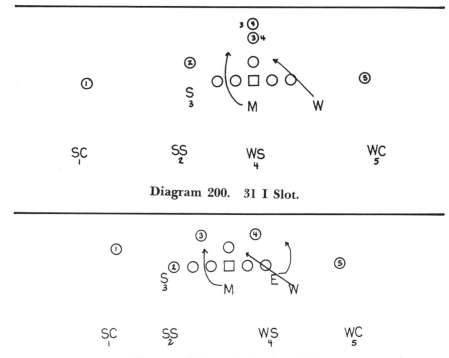

Diagram 199. 22 Flanker Split.

Diagram 200. 31 I Slot.

Diagram 201. 32 Flanker Split.

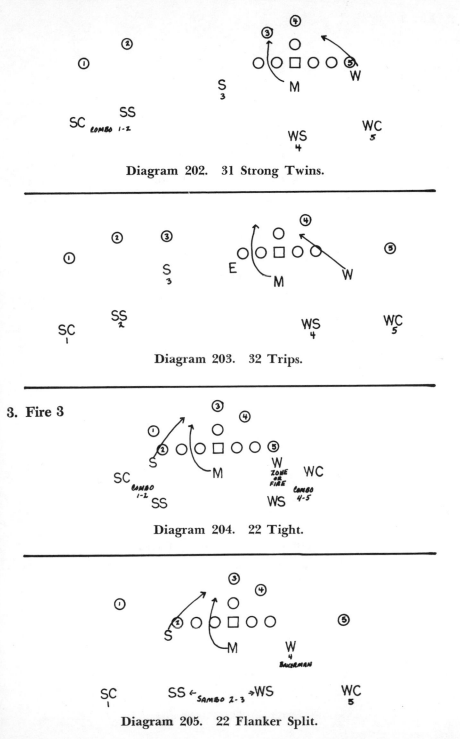

Diagram 202.   31 Strong Twins.

Diagram 203.   32 Trips.

3. Fire 3

Diagram 204.   22 Tight.

Diagram 205.   22 Flanker Split.

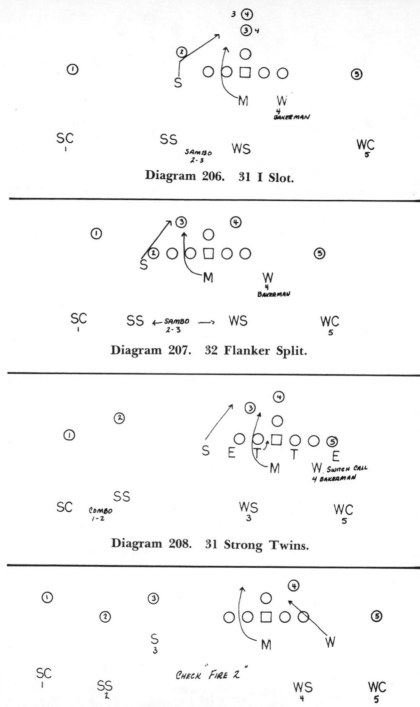

Diagram 206.   31 I Slot.

Diagram 207.   32 Flanker Split.

Diagram 208.   31 Strong Twins.

Diagram 209.   32 Trips.

4. Fire 4

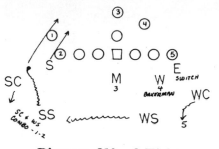

Diagram 210.   2 Tight.

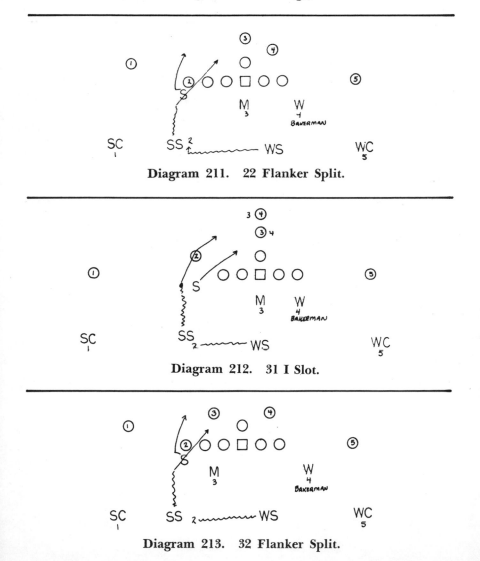

Diagram 211.   22 Flanker Split.

Diagram 212.   31 I Slot.

Diagram 213.   32 Flanker Split.

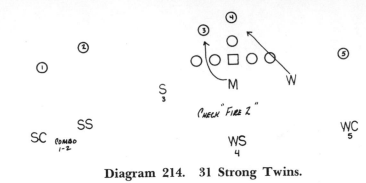

Diagram 214.   31 Strong Twins.

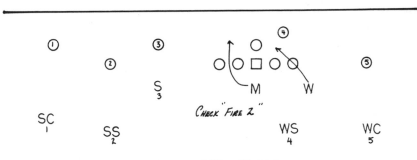

Diagram 215.   32 Trips.

5. Fire 5

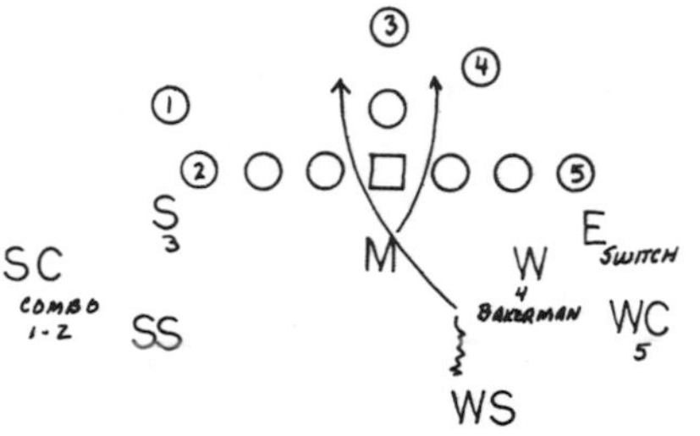

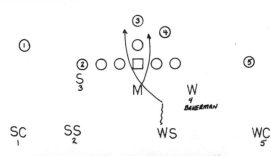

Diagram 216.   22 Tight.

Diagram 217.   22 Flanker Split.

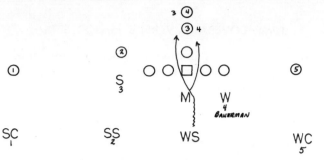

Diagram 218. 31 I Slot.

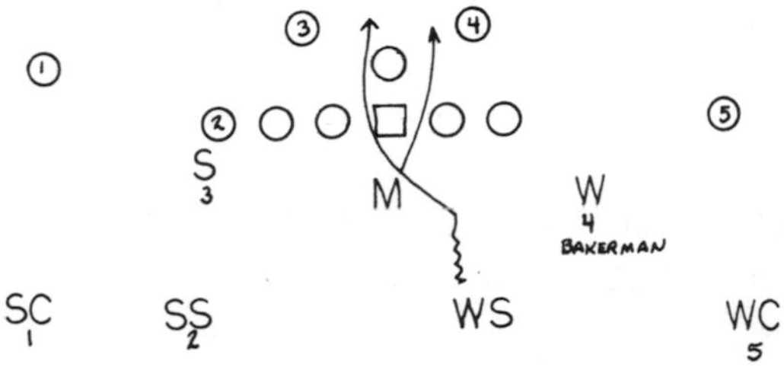

Diagram 219. 32 Flanker Split.

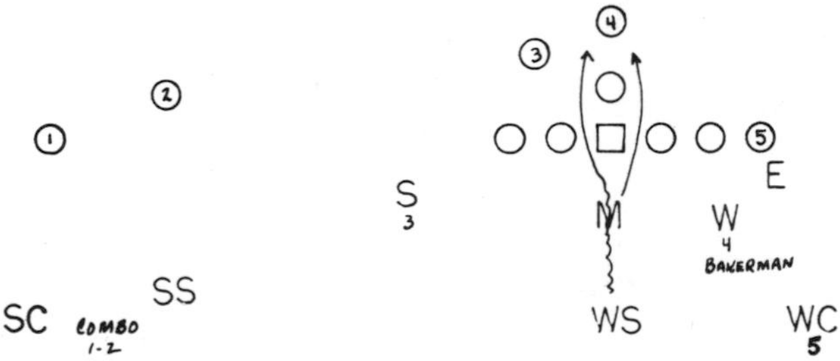

Diagram 220. 31 Strong Twins.

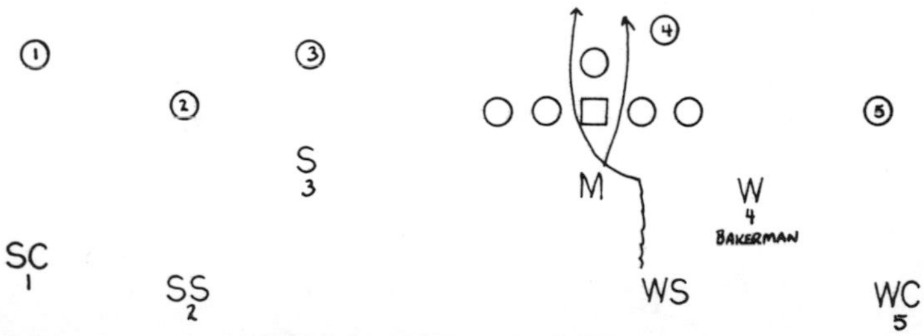

Diagram 221. 32 Trips.

JUMP COVERAGE VERSUS MAJOR SETS

Since, again, this is zone, I believe it is better understood by going over general rules. It is a three-deep zone pre-declared to either the strength or weakside of the offensive formation. This coverage is called in the following manner:

1. Strong Jump—pre-declared to strength of set.
2. Weak Jump—pre-declared to the weak side.
3. Jump to the Field—pre-declared in the huddle.
4. Jump to an Individual—make call after offense aligns.

Our strong safety makes a "me" or "you" call on Strong Jump and the weak safety does the same on a Weak Jump. These calls define who is going to cover the short ¼ of the field and be the forceman on the run. On a "me" call the safety takes these responsibilities; on a "you" call the corner performs these functions. The outside linebacker *away* from the call always covers the flat ¼ his side. See Diagrams #222 and #223.

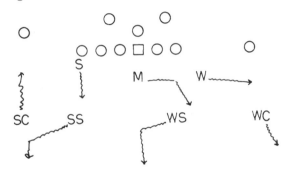

Diagram 222. You Call.

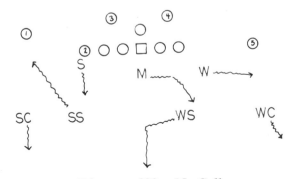

Diagram 223. Me Call.

Use three methods of "jumping."
1. Come up fast and try to "deck" the receiver.
2. Play two yards off receiver and use your hands on him.
3. Fake close coverage, then back off and level off on him 6 to 8 yards deep.

STRONG JUMP CALLED

Strong Corner

Get "You" call from S.S. Use one of techniques described above. Attempt to force receiver *inside*. If he persists in going outside, "flatten" him out. After you have done this, check #2 for run pass key. If #2 is blocking, become forceman. If #2 is off, you have flat ¼ on straight drop and sprint passes your way. If QB sprints away, look for throwback and "bracket" the ball.

Strong Safety

Give "You" call to corner. Don't allow wide eligible to get too wide on you. Cheat wide side off of hash marks. If eligible gets 12 yards or more change call to a "Me" call. On a "You" call on snap, move to outside deep ⅓. If QB is straight back or toward you, go to a position halfway between sideline and your hash mark. Keep all receivers inside and in front, unless you "lap" with the sideline. Never get closer to sideline than 8 yards. Key both #1 and #2 and the ball. Both must block before you support. If QB sprints away, revolve to flow keeping all receivers inside and in front of you. If QB pulls up, you pull up. Never get closer than 15 yards from your weak safety.

Weak Safety

Cheat to wide side of field off of the hash marks. On snap if QB is straight back, sprint to middle ⅓. Get to zone first then get depth. If QB sprints strong, sprint to the hash mark and then get depth. Do not cross hash until after the ball is released. Anytime QB pulls up, you pull up. Always keep a relative distance from your outside man. This about 15 yards. If QB sprints weak, do not cross your hash mark until ball is thrown. Key ball and uncovered linemen for run or pass indication.

Weak Corner

Same as Strong Corner on a "You" call. Remember that, if ball is on your hash mark and you get a strong sprint out, your zone increases. Bracket the ball but don't let any receiver outside of you. All 21 men in the game must be "inside" of you.

Sam

Play regular 43 keys for run. If a pass shows, you do the following. (Remember we jump on pass downs, so think pass first.)
1. QB straight back—force #2 outside if possible. Shuffle back to hook zone your side. You have hook-curl. Be aware that #3 may "leak" out late.
2. QB toward you—Harass #2, shuffle out and get width. Check containment. If needed come up and contain, if not get depth into your zone.
3. QB sprints away—While engaging #2, you will feel the flow away. If #2 makes an inside release, cover him short across as your zone has moved over due to the weak sprint out.

Mike

Play 43 keys for run. On pass show do the following:
1. Quarterback straight back—get to weak hook area. Know where you are on the field so you will know where the weak hook area is. See what #4 is doing. If #4 goes flat, help out on #5 curling by looking him up and driving underneath him.
2. QB sprints out weak side—check and see if our end has contained the sprint out. If not, help out on containment. If QB is contained get to curl area.
3. QB sprints out strong side—go to weak hook area and look for throwback if QB pulls up. If QB continues on, help on #5 on the curl.

Will

Align wider. On pass show do the following:
1. QB goes straight back—sprint to weak flat. Get 8-10 yards deep. Never get closer to sideline than 6 yards. Check #5 as you

go to your zone. If he clears, look up #4. You have #4 or #5 in the flat.

2. QB sprints out weak—check #4 first, then #5. By playing a cushion just ahead of #4 you can often be in the line of flight for #5 running a curl.

3. QB sprints out strong—start to weak flat. If QB keeps on sprinting strong, back up to area between your weak safety and weak corner.

Weak Jump Called (Diagram #224).

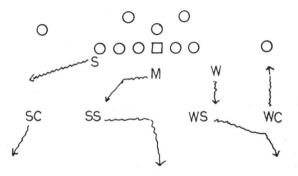

Diagram 224.

Weak Corner—Same as strong corner on strong jump.
Weak Safety—Same as strong safety on strong jump.
Strong Safety—Same as weak safety on strong jump.
Strong Corner—Same as weak corner on strong jump.
Sam—Same as Will on strong jump—start flat first, then determine run or pass.
Mike—Same as strong jump only you go to strong hook area.
Will—Same as Sam on strong jump.

8

Creating an Impenetrable 43 Defense

SPECIFICS OF EACH POSITION

We have already covered the specifics of all three linebackers in Chapter 3. Chapter 7 contains the specifics of the four secondary men. This only leaves the two tackles and two ends, which will be covered at this time.

Defensive Ends—Reading Techniques—43 Defense

Stance and Alignment. Three point stance with outside hand down and outside foot back. Cant slightly to the inside.

> NOTE: Strong Defensive End can square up and keep feet parallel. Inside foot should be in line with offensive tackles outside foot. Weight should be evenly distributed on down hand and balls of the feet.

Key. Offensive tackles head. If you have a tight end, you must "feel" him but continue to key the tackle.

Reactions to Your Key. O.T. (Offensive tackle).

Reach Blocks—Use hand shiver, keep outside leg free, shuffle out and pursue laterally versus run, rush in lanes versus sprint out pass. This key indicates Outside Play.

O.T. Turns Out—Use flipper, keep leverage on blocker, drive laterally to the inside turning blocker to the inside with you. This key indicates Inside Play.

O.T. Post Blocks—Use flipper and shoulder while stepping toward offensive tight end. Play through his angle block. If you get "hung up," split the seam or drop under both blocks, or spin against the power. This key indicates a Double Team Block.

O.T. Down Blocks on Your Tackle—First, brace for down block from offensive tight-end using outside shoulder flipper. If you don't "feel" this immediately, look for near back to lead on you. Step to the outside if this happens. If neither of these things happens, lead step to inside, stay square and close trap hole. This key can be one of three things: (1) Tear Sweep (2) Green Bay Sweep (3) Long Trap.

O.T. Releases Inside—Chase. This key indicates Running Play to the other side.

O.T. Pulls to Inside—Chase. This key indicates Trap or Sweep Away.

O.T. Pulls to Outside—Use Reach Techniques. This key indicates Outside Run Play.

O.T. Shows Pass—Rush from outside in. Break back on the draw by using reverse pivot.

   Escape Techniques.

Shoulder Slide—Earn a tie with blocker by meeting shoulder with shoulder and bringing up flipper. Keep leverage on blocker and slide against the power. Do not "run around" the power.

Shiver Shuffle—Strike blocker with butt of hands, keeping outside leg free. Shuffle in direction of blocker's head.

Hand Grab—Grasp the blocker's jersey with both hands. Hold firmly away from body and legs while reading flow. Pull him away from POA (point of attack) while you step towards POA.

Spin—Keep under-and-up leverage. Feel the angle block and pivot into it. Quickly square up and locate the ball.

   Pursuit.

After escaping blocker, take an intelligent path that will intercept the path of the ball while preventing cut backs. Never pursue on the inside arc. Give ground to maintain position on the ball.

   Pass Rush.

There Are Four Types of Pass Blocking:

1. *Rider.* This type will "set," engage you, stay in front of you, and go where you go. Against this type block you must use the Pressure Drive technique and overpower him.

2. *Pop, Recoil, and Ride.* This type blocker will set, deliver a blow, set again and then try to stay in front of you. When he Pops, he is extended and can be dodged. If he Pops and recoils, he is not in a power position and can be run over.

3. *Set and Cut.* This type block is vulnerable to head fakes and hand grabs. He wants you to use pressure drive so he can use your momentum to trip you with his cut block.

4. *Aggressive and Control.* This indicates a play action pass. Play him first for run, then use any of the escapes indicated above; arm swipes, hand grabs, spins, etc.

If we have called a stunt or blitz, use the pressure drive and try to get to blocker before he is set. Remember this simple axiom: When reading, use hands and arm extension; when blitzing or stunting, use shoulder and flipper.

Defensive Tackles—Reading Techniques—43 Defense

(a) *Stance and Alignment.* Four point stance head on the offensive guards. Vary depth off the ball. Play close on short yards, passing situations and when stunting. Play three feet off on all normal situations.

(b) *Key.* On 43 inside "feel" guard your side, but key center and off guard. On 43 outside key guard your side but "feel" what center and off guard are doing.

(c) *Charge.* 43 Inside—Step tough with inside foot first, then bring outside foot parallel. Use short steps. 43 Outside—Step tough with outside foot first, then bring inside foot parallel.

(d) *Reactions to Your Key.*

43 Inside (Key Center)

OC (Offensive Center) Reach Blocks on You—Same as reach key for the defensive end outlined above.

OC Turns Out on You—Use same reaction as described above for defensive ends versus turn out key. Key indicates a middle trap or run play away from you.

OC Angle Blocks on Our Other Tackle—Look for trap from off guard first. Step inside and stay square. Meet trapper with inside shoulder. Key also could indicate a sweep to your side, if this is true the offensive tackle your side will be down blocking on you. Since you must play the trap first, you will have lost position on the tackles block. You have only two choices (1) use hand grab and step inside tackle's angle block or (2) spin into tackle and regain leverage on the ball.

OC Shows Pass—Since you are in a reading defense, play through the offensive guard using hands and arm extension. Use techniques as outlined in *Pass Rush.* Do not pick gaps until draw possibility is gone. Keep pressing in lanes and get your hands up when QB draws back to throw.

43 Outside (Key Guard)

OG (Offensive Guard) Reach Blocks on You—Use techniques outlined above when our defensive end got a Reach Key from his tackle.

OG Turns Out on You—His head will tell you it is a turn out block—use "turn out" techniques described above. Key indicates middle trap or check back block.

OG Post Blocks on You—This is double team key. You must fight angle or power, block from either the center or offensive tackle. Step to power and beat it by quick recognition, or use escape techniques of split, spin or drop. 43 Outside makes you think of your outside hole first.

OG Pulls to the Inside—Step inside with inside foot, stay square and look for center's check back block. Mike should handle this, but play this as center's turn out block.

OG Pulls to the Outside—Check center first. He will be reaching on you or checking back. If he is reaching, use reach keys. If he is checking back, play sweep first then trap. Mike should have the trap.

OG Shows Pass—Same as 43 Inside.

Defensive Play Book 43 Defense Repertoire

FRONTS	COVERAGES
43 Inside	Blue, Jump, Orange, Gray, Blue Double
43 Outside	Blue, Jump, Orange, Gray, Blue Double
43 Pinch	Black, Orange
43 Over	Blue, Jump, Orange, Gray, Blue Double
43 Slant	Blue, Jump, Orange, Gray, Blue Double
43 Missouri	Blue
43 Mike Strong	Blue, Jump, Orange, Gray, Blue Double
43 Fire 1	Black
43 Fire 2	Black
43 Fire 3	Black-Bakerman
43 Fire 4	Black-Bakerman
43 Fire 5	Black-Bakerman
43 Fire 8	Orange

1. 43 Inside Vs. 22 Tight—Blue Coverage (Diagram #225).

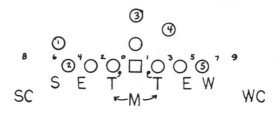

Diagram 225.

POS.	ALIGN.	KEY	RUN TO	PASS TO	ST. BACK	RUN AWAY	PASS AWAY
Sam	0	#2	6 Hole	#4 Rule	Banjo	Pursue	Banjo
SE	Outside	T	4 Hole	Rush	Rush	Chase	Chase
ST	Heads	Center	0 Hole	Rush	Rush-Draw	Pursue	Rush
Mike	Heads	#3	2-3 Holes	Zone	Banjo	Pursue	Banjo
WT	Heads	Center	1 Hole	Rush	Rush	Pursue	Rush
WE	Outside	T-#4	5 Hole	Rush	Rush	Chase	Chase
Will	0	#5	7 Hole	Contain	Zone	Pursue	Zone
SC	See above	#1 "You"	8 Hole	Combo	Combo	Bracket	Combo
SS	"	#2 "You"	6-8 Holes	"	"	"	"
WS	"	#5 "You"	7-9 Holes	"	"	"	"
WC	"	#4 "You"	9 Hole	"	"	"	"

2. 43 Inside Vs. 22 Flanker Split—Blue Coverage (Diagram #226).

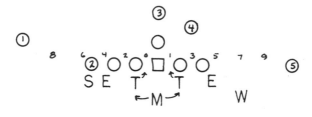

Diagram 226.

POS.	ALIGN.	KEY	RUN TO	PASS TO	ST. BACK	RUN AWAY	PASS AWAY
Sam	0	#2	6 Hole	#4 Rule	Banjo	Pursue	Banjo
SE	Outside	T	4 Hole	Rush	Rush	Chase	Chase
ST	Heads	Center	0 Hole	Rush	Rush	Pursue	Rush
Mike	Heads	#3	2-3 Holes	#3 Man	Banjo	Pursue	Banjo
WT	Heads	Center	1 Hole	Rush	Rush	Pursue	Rush
WE	Outside	T-#4	5 Hole	Contain	Rush	Chase	Chase
Will	Regular	T-#4	9 Hole	#4	#4	Pursue	#4-Zone
SC	See above	#1 "Me"	Support	#1 Man	#1 Man	Bracket	#1 Man
SS	"	#2 "Me"	8 Hole	#2 Man	#2-#3 Deep	"	#2-#3 Deep
WS	"	#4 "Me"	Support	Free	Free	Free	Free
WC	"	#5 "Me"	Support	#5 Man	#5 Man	Bracket	#5 Man

3. 43 Inside Vs. 31 I Slot—Blue Coverage (Diagram #227).

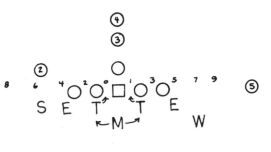

Diagram 227.

POS.	ALIGN.	KEY	RUN TO	PASS TO	ST. BACK	RUN AWAY	PASS AWAY
Sam	H	#2-Ball	6 Hole	#4 Rule	Free	Pursue	#2 Short
SE	Outside	T	4 Hole	Rush	Rush	Chase	Chase
ST	Heads	C	0 Hole	Rush	Rush	Pursue	Rush
Mike	Heads	#3	2-3 Holes	#3 Man	#3 Man	Pursue	#3 Man
WT	Heads	C	1 Hole	Rush	Rush	Pursue	Rush
WE	Outside	T	5 Hole	Rush	Contain	Chase	Chase
Will	0	#5	7 Hole	Contain	#4 Man	Pursue	#4 Zone
SC	See above	#1 Me	Support	#1 Man	#1 Man	Bracket	#1 Man
SS	"	#2 Me	8 Hole	Sambo	Sambo	"	#2 Deep
WS	"	#3 You	Support	Combo	Sambo	"	Sambo
WC	"	#5 You	9 Hole	Combo	#5 Man	"	#5 Man

4. 43 Inside Vs. 32 Flanker Split—Blue Coverage (Diagram #228).

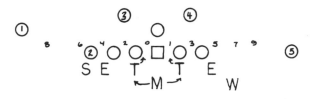

Diagram 228.

POS.	ALIGN.	KEY	RUN TO	PASS TO	ST. BACK	RUN AWAY	PASS AWAY
Sam	H	#2	6 Hole	#4 Rule	Banjo	Pursue	Banjo
SE	Outside	T	4 Hole	Rush	Contain	Chase	Chase
ST	Heads	C	0 Hole	Rush	Rush	Pursue	Rush
Mike	Heads	#3	2-3 Holes	Zone	Banjo	Pursue	Banjo
WT	Heads	C	1 Hole	Rush	Rush	Pursue	Rush
WE	Outside	T-#4	5-7 Holes	Contain	Contain	Chase	Chase
Will	Regular	#4	9 Hole	#4	#4	Pursue	#4 Zone

POS.	ALIGN.	KEY	RUN TO	PASS TO	ST. BACK	RUN AWAY	PASS AWAY
SC	See above	#1 Me	Support	#1 Man	#1 Man	Bracket	#1 Man
SS	"	#2 Me	8 Hole	Sambo	#2-#3 Deep	"	#2-#3 Deep
WS	"	#4 Me	Support	Free	Free	"	Sambo
WC	"	#5 Me	Support	#5 Man	#5 Man	"	#5 Man

5. 43 Inside Vs. 32 Trips—Blue Coverage (Diagram #229).

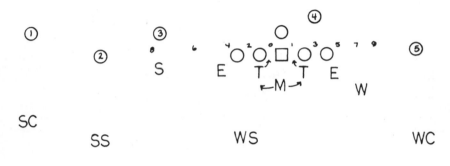

Diagram 229.

POS.	ALIGN.	KEY	RUN TO	PASS TO	ST. BACK	RUN AWAY	PASS AWAY
Sam	On #3	#3	6 Hole	#3 Man	#3 Man	Pursue	#3 Man
SE	Outside	T	4 Hole	Contain	Contain	Chase	Chase
ST	Heads	C	0-Hole	Rush	Rush	Pursue	Rush
Mike	Heads	Ball	2-3 Holes	Zone	Zone	Pursue	Zone
WT	Heads	C	1 Hole	Rush	Rush	Pursue	Rush
WE	Outside	T-#4	5 Hole	Contain	Contain	Chase	Chase
Will	Regular	#4	7-4 Holes	#4	#4	Pursue	#4 Zone
SC	On #1	#1 Me	Support	#1	#1	Bracket	#1
SS	On #2	#2 Me	8 Hole	#2	#2	"	#2
WS	Mid 3-4	#3-#4	Support	Free	Free	"	Free
WC	On #5	#5	Support	#5	#5	"	#5

6. 43 Outside Vs. All Sets (Diagram #230).

Diagram 230.

NOTE: On all 43 Outside defenses, versus all sets the only change comes in the three middle men—the two tackles and Mike. For that reason we will only cover their responsibilities. Everyone else is the same as previously described.

POS.	ALIGN.	KEY	RUN TO	PASS TO	ST. BACK	RUN AWAY	PASS AWAY
ST	Heads	G	2 Hole	Rush	Rush	Pursue	Rush
Mike	Heads	C-#3	0-1 Holes		Same As 43 Inside		
WT	Heads	G	3 Hole	Rush	Rush	Pursue	Rush

7. 43 Over Vs. All Sets (Diagram #231).

Diagram 231.

NOTE: This defense again only envolves the three middle men.

POS.	ALIGN.	KEY	RUN TO	PASS TO	ST. BACK	RUN AWAY	PASS AWAY
ST	Outside C	C	0 Hole				
Mike	Outside G	G	2 Hole		All The Same As 43 Inside		
WT	Heads	G	1-3 Holes				

NOTE: Over call be called strong or weak.

8. 43 Slant Vs. All Sets (Diagram #232).

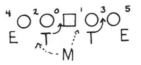

Diagram 232.

NOTE: Again this defense pertains only to the three middle men. Also there is no reason to chart it because it is simply moving into an Over *after* the snap.

9. 43 Pinch Vs. All Sets (Diagram #233).

NOTE: This is a special defense, and is used mostly on short yardage. It is played with Black Coverage. I don't think it is necessary to graph it against all sets as Black Coverage will be diagramed on the fires or blitzes.

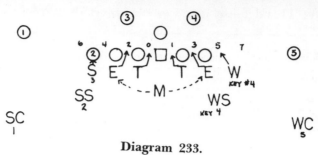

Diagram 233.

Sam	Aligns heads on #2. Plays him tough and limits the 4 hole but has #3 man on pass show.
SE	Tough in the 2 hole.
ST	Tough in the 0 hole.
Mike	Aligns heads on center but is deeper and has the 4-5 holes.
WT	Tough in the 1 hole.
WE	Tough in the 3 hole.
Will	Aligns close has 5-7 hole and #4 on passes.
Secondary	Plays Black.

10. 43 Missouri Vs. 22 Tight—Blue Coverage (Diagram #234).

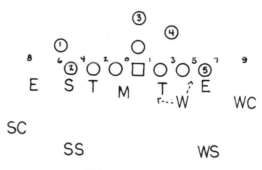

Diagram 234.

POS.	ALIGN.	KEY	RUN TO	PASS TO	ST. BACK	RUN AWAY	PASS AWAY
Sam	Heads	#2	4-6 Holes	#3 Man	#3 Man	Pursue	#3-Zone
SE	60	#3-Ball	6-8 Holes	Contain	Contain	Chase	Chase
ST	Heads	T	2-4 Holes	Rush	Rush	Pursue	Rush
Mike	0 Hole	C-G	0 Hole	Rush	Rush	Pursue	Rush
WT	Outside Ear	G	3 Hole	Rush	Rush	Pursue	Rush
WE	Switch	#5	7 Hole	Contain	Contain	Chase	Chase
Will	Heads	T-4-Ball	1-5 Holes	#4	#4	Pursue	#4-Zone
SC	See above	#1 You	Support	Combo	Combo	Bracket	Combo
SS	”	#1-#2 You	”	Combo	Combo	”	Combo
WS	”	#4 You	”	Combo	Combo	”	Combo
WC	”	#5 You	9 Hole	Combo	Combo	”	Combo

11. 43 Missouri Vs. 22 Flanker Split—Blue Coverage (Diagram #235).

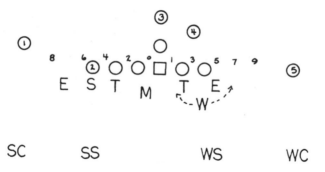

Diagram 235.

POS.	ALIGN.	KEY	RUN TO	PASS TO	ST. BACK	RUN AWAY	PASS AWAY
Sam	Heads	#2	4-6 Holes	#3 Man	#3 Man	Pursue	#3 Zone
SE	60	#3-Ball	6-8 Holes	Contain	Contain	Chase	Chase
ST	Heads	T	2-4 Holes	Rush	Rush	Pursue	Rush
Mike	0 Hole	C-G	0 Hole	Rush	Rush	Pursue	Rush
WT	Outside Ear	G	3 Hole	Rush	Rush	Pursue	Rush
WE	Outside	T-#4	5 Hole	Contain	Contain	Chase	Chase
Will	Heads	T-4-Ball	1-7 Holes	#4	#4	Pursue	#4 Zone
SC	On #1	#1-Me	Support	#1 Man	#1 Man	Bracket	#1 Man
SS	On #2	#2-Me	Support	#2 Man	#2 Man	Bracket	#2 Man
WS	Outside #4	#4-Me	″	Free	Free	″	Free
WC	On #5	#5-Me	″	#5 Man	#5 Man	″	#5 Man

12. 43 Missouri Vs. 31 I Slot—Blue Coverage (Diagram #236).

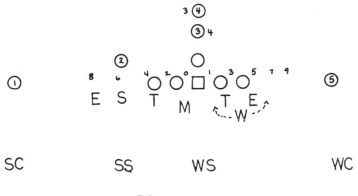

Diagram 236.

POS.	ALIGN.	KEY	RUN TO	PASS TO	ST. BACK	RUN AWAY	PASS AWAY
Sam	Heads	#2	4-6 Holes	#3	#3	Pursue	#3-Zone
SE	60	#2	6-8 Holes	Contain	Contain	Chase	Chase
ST	Heads	T	2-4 Holes	Rush	Rush	Pursue	Rush
Mike	0 Hole	C-G	0 Hole	Rush	Rush	Pursue	Rush

POS.	ALIGN.	KEY	RUN TO	PASS TO	ST. BACK	RUN AWAY	PASS AWAY
WT	Outside Ear	G	3 Hole	Rush	Rush	Pursue	Rush
WE	Switch	#5	7 Hole	Contain	Contain	Chase	Chase
Will	Heads	T-4 Ball	1-5 Holes	Zone	Zone	Pursue	#4 Zone
SC	On #1	#1 Me	Support	#1	#1	Bracket	#1
SS	On #2	#2 Me	Support	#2	#2	"	#2
WS	Center	#4 You	"	Combo	Combo	"	Free
WC	See above	#5 You	9 Hole	Combo	Combo	"	#5

13. 43 Missouri Vs. 32 Flanker Split—Blue Coverage (Diagram #237).

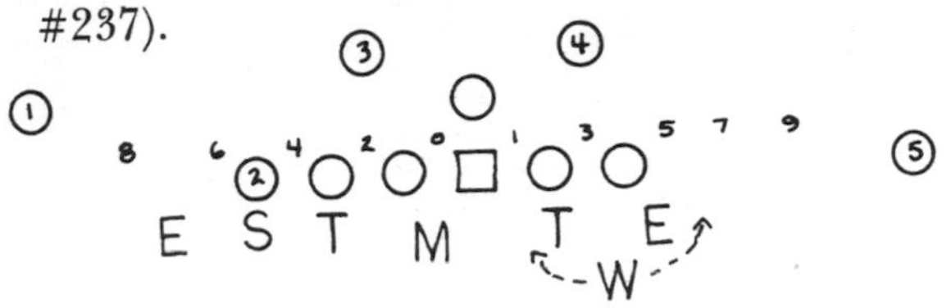

Diagram 237.

POS.	ALIGN.	KEY	RUN TO	PASS TO	ST. BACK	RUN AWAY	PASS AWAY
Sam	Heads	#2	4-6 Holes	Banjo/SS	Banjo/SS	Pursue	Banjo/SS
SE	60	#3-Ball	6-8 Holes	Contain	Contain	Chase	Chase
ST	Heads	T	4-2 Holes	Rush	Rush	Pursue	Rush
Mike	0 Hole	C-G	0 Hole	Rush	Rush	Pursue	Rush
WT	Outside Ear	G	3 Hole	Rush	Rush	Pursue	Rush
WE	Outside	T-4	5 Hole	Contain	Contain	Chase	Chase
Will	Heads	T-4 Ball	1-7 Holes	#4	#4	Pursue	#4-Zone
SC	On #1	#1 Mc	Support	#1	#1	Bracket	#1
SS	On #2	#2 Me	Support	Banjo/Sam	Banjo/Sam	Bracket	Banjo/Sam
WS	Outside #4	#4 Me	7-9 Holes	Free	Free	Bracket	Free
WC	On #5	#5 Me	Support	#5	#5	Bracket	#5

14. Missouri Vs. 32 Trips—Blue Coverage (Diagram #238).

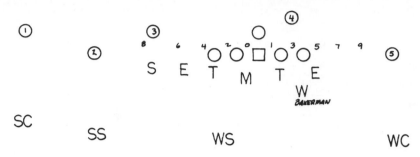

Diagram 238.

POS.	ALIGN.	KEY	RUN TO	PASS TO	ST. BACK	RUN AWAY	PASS AWAY
Sam	On #3	#3	6-8 Holes	#3	#3	Pursue	#3
SE	See above	#3-Ball	4-6 Holes	Contain	Contain	Chase	Chase
ST	Heads	T	4-2 Holes	Rush	Rush	Pursue	Rush
Mike	0 Hole	G-C	0 Hole	Rush	Rush	Pursue	Rush
WT	Heads	G	3 Hole	Rush	Rush	Pursue	Rush
WE	Outside	T-4 Ball	5 Hole	Contain	Contain	Chase	Chase
Will	Heads	T-4 Ball	1-7 Holes	Bakerman	Bakerman	Pursue	Bakerman
SC	On #1	#1 Me	Support	#1	#1	Bracket	#1
SS	On #2	#2 Me	Support	#2	#2	Bracket	#2
WS	Mid 3-4	#4	Support	Free	Free	Bracket	Free
WC	On #5	#5	Support	#5	#5	Bracket	#5

15. 43 Mike Strong Vs. All Sets (Diagram #239).

NOTE: This is just 43 Inside with the Mike and Will line-backers moved over to the strong side. All rules against all sets remain the same as 43 Inside.

Diagram 239.

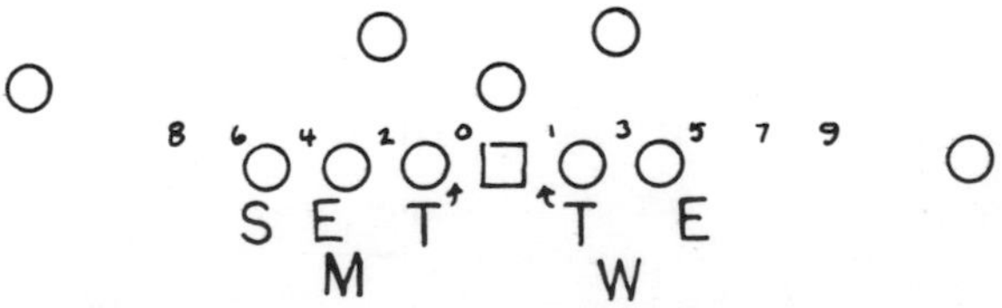

16. 43 Fire 1 Vs. 22 Tight—Black Coverage (Diagram #240).

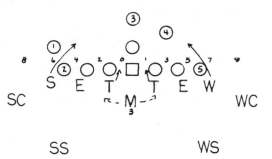

Diagram 240.

POS.	ALIGN.	KEY	RUN TO	PASS TO	ST. BACK	RUN AWAY	PASS AWAY
Sam	0	#2 In-Out	6 Hole	Contain	Contain	Chase	Chase
SE	Outside	T-Hard	4 Hole	Rush	Rush	Pursue	Rush
ST	Heads	C-Hard	0 Hole	Rush	Rush	Pursue	Rush
Mike	Heads	#3	2-3 Holes	#3	#3	Pursue	#3
WT	Heads	C-Hard	1 Hole	Rush	Rush	Pursue	Rush
WE	Outside	T-Hard	5 Hole	Rush	Rush	Pursue	Rush
Will	0	#5 In-Out	7 Hole	Contain	Contain	Chase	Chase
SC	See above	#1 You	8 Hole	Combo	Combo	Bracket	Combo
SS	"	#2 You	Support	Combo	Combo	Bracket	Combo
WS	"	#4 You	Support	Combo	Combo	Bracket	Combo
WC	"	#5 You	9 Hole	Combo	Combo	Bracket	Combo

17. 43 Fire 1 Vs. 22 Flanker Split—Black Coverage (Diagram #241).

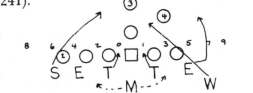

Diagram 241.

POS.	ALIGN.	KEY	RUN TO	PASS TO	ST. BACK	RUN AWAY	PASS AWAY
Sam	0	#2 In-Out	6 Hole	Contain	Contain	Chase	Chase
SE	Outside	T-Hard	4 Hole	Rush	Rush	Pursue	Rush
ST	Heads	C-Hard	0 Hole	Rush	Rush	Pursue	Rush
Mike	Heads	#3	2-3 Holes	#3	#3	Pursue	#3
WT	Heads	C-Hard	1 Hole	Rush	Rush	Pursue	Rush
WE	Outside	Stunt	7 Hole	Contain	Contain	Chase	Chase
Will	Regular	Stunt	5 Hole	Rush	Rush	Pursue	Rush
SC	See above	#1 Me	Support	#1	#1	Bracket	#1
SS	See above	#2 Me	8 Hole	#2	#2	Bracket	#2
WS	See above	#4	Support	#4	#4	Bracket	#4
WC	See above	#5	Support	#5	#5	Bracket	#5

18. 43 Fire 1 Vs. 31 I Slot—Black Coverage (Diagram #242).

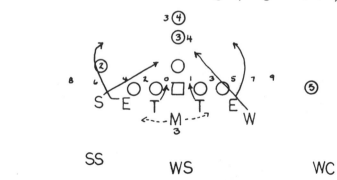

Diagram 242.

POS.	ALIGN.	KEY	RUN TO	PASS TO	ST. BACK	RUN AWAY	PASS AWAY
Sam	H	Stunt	4 Hole	Rush	Rush	Pursue	Rush
SE	Outside	Stunt	6 Hole	Contain	Contain	Chase	Chase
ST	Heads	C Hard	0 Hole	Rush	Rush	Pursue	Rush
Mike	Heads	#3	2-3 Holes	#3	#3	Pursue	#3
WT	Heads	C Hard	1 Hole	Rush	Rush	Pursue	Rush

POS.	ALIGN.	KEY	RUN TO	PASS TO	ST. BACK	RUN AWAY	PASS AWAY
WE	Outside	T Hard	5 Hole	Rush	Rush	Pursue	Rush
Will	0	#5 Hard	7 Hole	Contain	Rush	Chase	Chase
SC	See above	#1 Me	Support	#1	#1	Bracket	#1
SS	See above	#2 Me	8 Hole	#2	#2	Bracket	#2
WS	See above	#4	Support	Combo	Combo	Bracket	Combo Free
WC	See above	#5	9 Hole	Combo	Combo	Bracket	Combo #5

19. 43 Fire 1 Vs. 32 Flanker Split—Black Coverage (Diagram #243).

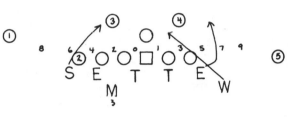

Diagram 243.

NOTE: Over Call by Mike.

POS.	ALIGN.	KEY	RUN TO	PASS TO	ST. BACK	RUN AWAY	PASS AWAY
Sam	"0"	#2	6 Hole	Contain	Contain	Chase	Chase
SE	Outside	T	4 Hole	Rush	Rush	Pursue	Rush
ST	Outside C	C	0 Hole	Rush	Rush	Pursue	Rush
Mike	Outside G	G	2 Hole	#3	#3	Pursue	#3
WT	Heads	G	1-3 Holes	Rush	Rush	Pursue	Rush
WE	Outside	Stunt	7 Hole	Contain	Contain	Chase	Chase
Will	Regular	Stunt	5 Hole	Rush	Rush	Pursue	Rush
SC	On #1	#1 Me	Support	#1	#1	Bracket	#1
SS	On #2	#2 Me	8 Hole	#2	#2	Bracket	#2
WS	On #4	#4 Me	9 Hole	#4	#4	Bracket	#4
WC	On #5	#5 Me	Support	#5	#5	Bracket	#5

20. 43 Fire 1 Vs. 32 Trips—Black Coverage (Diagram #244).

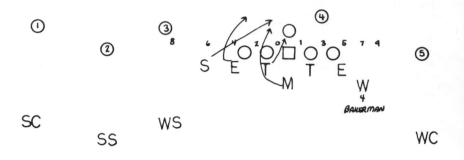

Diagram 244.

NOTE: **One of** the advantages of our blitzing system was the ability to change the blitz at the line of scrimmage. Against this set it is obvious that Mike can't cover #3. Also the best blitz here is to the open side. The procedure here was to check to a Fire 3. We simply hollered "Check 3."

POS.	ALIGN.	KEY	RUN TO	PASS TO	ST. BACK	RUN AWAY	PASS AWAY
Sam	Split Rule	Stunt	4 Hole	Rush	Rush	Pursue	Rush
SE	Outside	Stunt	6 Hole	Contain	Contain	Chase	Chase
ST	Heads	Stunt	0 Hole	Rush	Rush	Pursue	Rush
Mike	Heads	Stunt	2 Hole	Rush	Rush	Pursue	Rush
WT	Heads	G-Spy	1-3 Holes	Spy	Spy	Pursue	Spy
WE	Outside	T-4	5 Hole	Contain	Contain	Chase	Chase
Will	Regular	#4	7-9 Holes	Bakerman	Bakerman	Pursue	Bakerman
SC	On #1	#1 Me	Support	#1	#1	Bracket	#1
SS	On #2	#2 Me	8 Hole	#2	#2	Bracket	#2
WS	Delay-#3	#3	Support	#3	#3	Bracket	#3
WC	On #5	#5	Support	#5	#5	#5	#5

21. 43 Fire 2 Vs. 22 Tight—Black Coverage (Diagram #245).

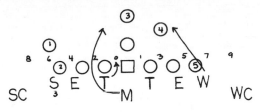

Diagram 245.

POS.	ALIGN.	KEY	RUN TO	PASS TO	ST. BACK	RUN AWAY	PASS AWAY
Sam	"0"	#2-#3	6 Hole	#4 Rule	#3	Pursue	#3-Zone
SE	Outside	T	4 Hole	Rush	Contain	Chase	Chase
ST	Heads	Stunt	0 Hole	Rush	Rush	Pursue	Rush
Mike	Heads	Stunt	2 Hole	Rush	Rush	Pursue	Rush
WT	Heads	G	1-3 Holes	Spy	Spy	Pursue	Spy
WE	Outside	T	5 Hole	Rush	Rush	Pursue	Rush
Will	"0"	Fire	7 Hole	Contain	Contain	Chase	Chase
SC	See above	#1 You	8 Hole	Combo	Combo	Bracket	Combo
SS	See above	#2 You	Support	Combo	Combo	Bracket	Combo
WS	See above	#4 You	Support	Combo	Combo	Bracket	Combo
WC	See above	#5 You	9 Hole	Combo	Combo	Bracket	Combo

22. 43 Fire 2 Vs. 22 Flanker Split—Black Coverage (Diagram #246).

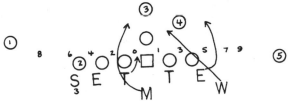

Diagram 246.

POS.	ALIGN.	KEY	RUN TO	PASS TO	ST. BACK	RUN AWAY	PASS AWAY
Sam	0	#2-#3	6 Hole	#4 Rule	#3	Pursue	#3
SE	Outside	T	4 Hole	Rush	Contain	Chase	Chase
ST	Heads	Stunt	0 Hole	Rush	Rush	Pursue	Rush
Mike	Heads	Stunt	2 Hole	Rush	Rush	Pursue	Rush
WT	Heads	G	1-3 Holes	Spy	Spy	Pursue	Spy
WE	Outside	Stunt	7 Hole	Contain	Contain	Chase	Chase
Will	Regular	Stunt	5 Hole	Rush	Rush	Pursue	Rush
SC	On #1	#1 Me	Support	#1	#1	Bracket	#1
SS	On #2	#2 Me	8 Hole	#2	#2	Bracket	#2
WS	On #4	#4 Me	9 Hole	#4	#4	Bracket	#4
WC	On #5	#5 Me	Support	#5	#5	Bracket	#5

23. 43 Fire 2 Vs. 31 I Slot—Black Coverage (Diagram #247).

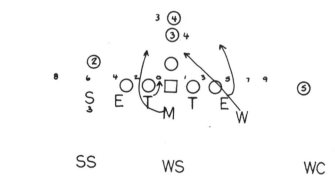

Diagram 247.

POS.	ALIGN.	KEY	RUN TO	PASS TO	ST. BACK	RUN AWAY	PASS AWAY
Sam	H	#2-#3	6 Hole	#4 Rule	#3	Pursue	#3 Zone
SE	Outside	T	4 Hole	Rush	Contain	Chase	Chase
ST	Heads	Stunt	0 Hole	Rush	Rush	Pursue	Rush
Mike	Heads	Stunt	2 Hole	Rush	Rush	Pursue	Rush
WT	Heads	G	1-3 Holes	Spy	Spy	Spy	Spy
WE	Outside	T	5 Hole	Rush	Rush	Pursue	Rush
Will	0	#5	7 Hole	Contain	Contain	Chase	Chase
SC	On #1	#1 Me	Support	#1	#1	Bracket	#1
SS	On #2	#2 Me	8 Hole	Sambo	#2	"	#2
WS	Middle	#4 You	Support	Combo	Combo	"	Sambo
WC	See above	#5 You	9 Hole	Combo	Combo	"	#5

24. 43 Fire 2 Vs. 32 Flanker Split—Black Coverage (Diagram #248).

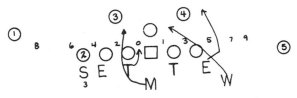

Diagram 248.

POS.	ALIGN.	KEY	RUN TO	PASS TO	ST. BACK	RUN AWAY	PASS AWAY
Sam	H	#2-#3	6 Hole	#4 Rule	#3	Pursue	#3
SE	Outside	T	4 Hole	Rush	Rush	Chase	Chase
ST	Heads	Stunt	0 Hole	Rush	Rush	Pursue	Rush
Mike	Heads	Stunt	2 Hole	''	''	''	''
WT	Heads	G	1-3 Holes	Spy	Spy	''	Spy
WE	Outside	Stunt (#4)	7 Hole	Contain	Contain	Chase	Chase
Will	Regular	Stunt (T)	5 Hole	Rush	Rush	Pursue	Rush
SC	On #1	#1 Me	Support	#1	#1	Bracket	#1
SS	On #2	#2 Me	8 Hole	#4 Rule Sambo	#2	Bracket	#2
WS	On #4	#4 Me	9 Hole	#4	#4	Bracket	#4 Rule Sambo
WC	On #5	#5 Me	Support	#5	#5	Bracket	#5

25. 43 Fire 2 32 Trips—Black Coverage (Diagram #249).

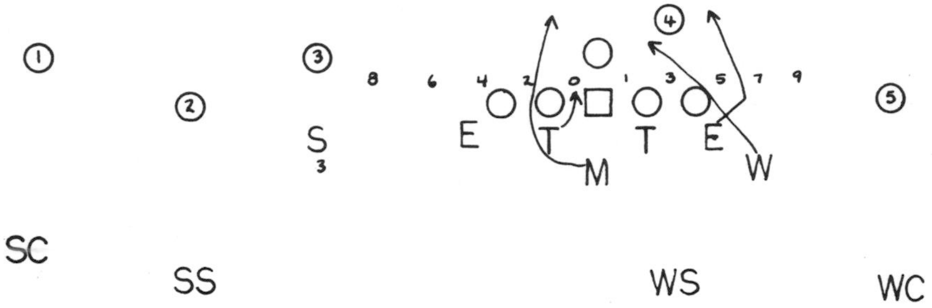

Diagram 249.

POS.	ALIGN.	KEY	RUN TO	PASS TO	ST. BACK	RUN AWAY	PASS AWAY
Sam	On #3	#3	6 Hole	#3	#3	Pursue	#3
SE	Outside	T	4 Hole	Contain	Contain	Chase	Chase
ST	Heads	Stunt	0 Hole	Rush	Rush	Pursue	Rush
Mike	Heads	Stunt	2 Hole	Rush	Rush	Pursue	Rush
WT	Heads	G	1-3 Holes	Spy	Spy	Pursue	Spy

POS.	ALIGN.	KEY	RUN TO	PASS TO	ST. BACK	RUN AWAY	PASS AWAY
WE	Outside	Stunt #4	7 Hole	Contain	Contain	Chase	Chase
Will	Regular	Stunt T	5 Hole	Rush	Rush	Pursue	Rush
SC	On #1	#1 Me	Support	#1	#1	Bracket	#1
SS	On #2	#2 Me	8 Hole	#2	#2	Bracket	#2
WS	On #4	#4 Me	9 Hole	#4	#4	Bracket	#4
WC	On #5	#5 Mc	Support	#5	#5	Bracket	#5

NOTE: There is a code word under Sam's rules, #4 Rule." This means that Sam does not contain (when he is not blitzing) unless both #3 and #4 come his way. If only #3 comes, Sam continues to stay in the pass defense. When #4 comes strong, then Sam knows there will be a Sambo on #2 and #3, and he is free to contain or force.

26. 43 Fire 3 Vs. 22 Tight—Black Coverage (Diagram #250).

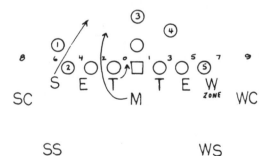

Diagram 250.

POS.	ALIGN.	KEY	RUN TO	PASS TO	ST. BACK	RUN AWAY	PASS AWAY
Sam	0	Fire	6 Hole	Contain	Contain	Chase	Chase
SE	Outside	T	4 Hole	Rush	Rush	Pursue	Rush
ST	Heads	Stunt	0 Hole	Rush	Rush	Pursue	Rush
Mike	Heads	Stunt	2 Hole	Rush	Rush	Pursue	Rush
WT	Heads	G	1-3 Holes	Spy	Spy	Pursue	Spy
WE	Outside	T	5 Hole	Rush	Contain	Chase	Chase
Will	0	#5	7 Hole	Contain	Zone	Pursue	Zone
SC	See above	#1 You	8 Hole	Combo	Combo	Bracket	Combo
SS	See above	#2 You	Support	Combo	Combo	Bracket	Combo
WS	See above	#4 You	Support	Combo	Combo	Bracket	Combo
WC	See above	#5 You	9 Hole	Combo	Combo	Bracket	Combo

27. 43 Fire 3 Vs. 22 Flanker Split—Black Coverage (Diagram #251).

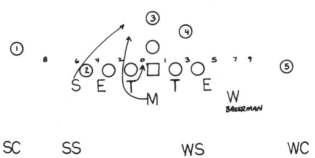

Diagram 251.

POS.	ALIGN.	KEY	RUN TO	PASS TO	ST. BACK	RUN AWAY	PASS AWAY
Sam	0	Fire	6 Hole	Contain	Contain	Chase	Chase
SE	Outside	T	4 Hole	Rush	Rush	Pursue	Rush
ST	Heads	Stunt	0 Hole	Rush	Rush	Pursue	Rush
Mike	Heads	Stunt	2 Hole	Rush	Rush	Pursue	Rush
WT	Heads	G	1-3 Holes	Spy	Spy	Pursue	Spy

POS.	ALIGN.	KEY	RUN TO	PASS TO	ST. BACK	RUN AWAY	PASS AWAY
WE	Outside	T-4	5 Hole	Contain	Contain	Chase	Chase
Will	Regular	#4	7-9 Holes	Bakerman	Bakerman	Pursue	Bakerman
SC	On #1	#1 Me	Support	#1	#1	Bracket	#1
SS	On #2	#2 Me	8 Hole	Sambo	Sambo	Bracket	Sambo
WS	#3 Late	#2-#3	Support	Sambo	Sambo	Bracket	Sambo
WC	On #5	#5	Support	#5	#5	Bracket	#5

28. 43 Fire 3 Vs. 31 I Slot—Black Coverage (Diagram #252).

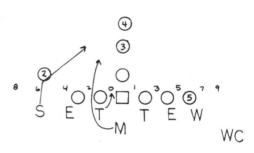

Diagram 252.

POS.	ALIGN.	KEY	RUN TO	PASS TO	ST. BACK	RUN AWAY	PASS AWAY
Sam	H	Fire	6 Hole	Contain	Contain	Chase	Chase
SE	Outside	T	4 Hole	Rush	Rush	Pursue	Rush
ST	Heads	Stunt	0 Hole	Rush	Rush	Pursue	Rush
Mike	Heads	Stunt	2 Hole	Rush	Rush	Pursue	Rush
WT	Heads	G	1-3 Holes	Spy	Spy	Pursue	Spy
WE	Outside	T	5 Hole	Rush	Contain	Chase	Chase
Will	0	Fire	7 Hole	Contain	Bakerman	Pursue	Bakerman
SC	#1	#1 Me	Support	#1	#1	Bracket	#1
SS	#2	#2 Me	8 Hole	Sambo	Sambo	Bracket	Sambo
WS	Middle	#4 You	Support	Combo	Sambo	Bracket	Sambo
WC	#5	#5 You	9 Hole	Combo	#5	Bracket	#5

29. 43 Fire 3 Vs. 32 Flanker Split—Black Coverage (Diagram #253).

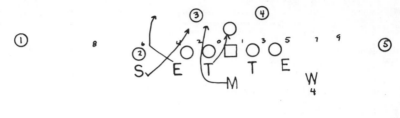

Diagram 253.

POS.	ALIGN.	KEY	RUN TO	PASS TO	ST. BACK	RUN AWAY	PASS AWAY
Sam	H	Stunt	4 Hole	Rush	Rush	Pursue	Rush
SE	Outside	Stunt	6 Hole	Contain	Contain	Chase	Chase
ST	Heads	Stunt	0 Hole	Rush	Rush	Pursue	Rush
Mike	Heads	Stunt	2 Hole	Rush	Rush	Pursue	Rush
WT	Heads	G	1-3 Holes	Spy	Spy	Pursue	Spy
WE	Outside	T	5 Hole	Contain	Contain	Chase	Chase
Will	Regular	#4	7 Hole	Bakerman	Bakerman	Pursue	Bakerman
SC	#1	#1 Me	Support	#1	#1	Bracket	#1
SS	#2	#2 Me	8 Hole	Sambo	Sambo	Bracket	Sambo
WS	#3 Late	#2-#3	Support	Sambo	Sambo	Bracket	Sambo
WC	#5	#5	Support	#5	#5	Bracket	#5

30. 43 Fire 3 Vs. 32 Trips—See #20 this chapter.

31. 43 Fire 4 Vs. 22 Tight—Black Coverage (Diagram #254).

Diagram 254.

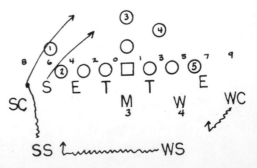

POS.	ALIGN.	KEY	RUN TO	PASS TO	ST. BACK	RUN AWAY	PASS AWAY
Sam	0	Fire	6 Hole	Rush	Rush	Pursue	Rush
SE	Outside	T	4 Hole	Rush	Rush	Pursue	Rush
ST	Heads	C	0 Hole	Rush	Rush	Pursue	Rush
Mike	Heads	#3	2-3 Holes	#3	#3	Pursue	#3
WT	Heads	C	1 Hole	Rush	Rush	Pursue	Rush
WE	Switch	#5	7 Hole	Contain	Contain	Chase	Chase
Will	Switch	T-#4	5 Hole	Bakerman	Bakerman	Pursue	Bakerman
SC	See above	#1-#2	Support	Combo	Combo	Bracket	Combo
SS	See above	Fire	8 Hole	Contain	Contain	Chase	Chase
WS	See above	#1-#2	Support	Combo/SC	Combo/SC	Bracket	Combo/SC
WC	See above	#5	9 Hole	#5	#5	Bracket	#5

32. 43 Fire 4 Vs. 22 Flanker Split—Black Coverage (Diagram #255).

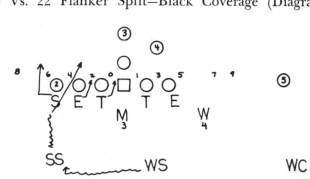

Diagram 255.

POS.	ALIGN.	KEY	RUN TO	PASS TO	ST. BACK	RUN AWAY	PASS AWAY
Sam	0	Stunt	6-8 Holes	Contain	Contain	Chase	Chase
SE	Heads	Fire	2 Hole	Rush	Rush	Pursue	Rush
ST	Heads	C	0 Hole	Rush	Rush	Pursue	Rush
Mike	Heads	#3	3-Free	#3	#3	Pursue	#3
WT	Heads	C	1 Hole	Rush	Rush	Pursue	Rush
WE	Outside	T-4	5 Hole	Contain	Contain	Chase	Chase
Will	Regular	#4	7-9 Holes	Bakerman	Bakerman	Pursue	Bakerman
SC	#1	#1 Me	Support	#1	#1	Bracket	#1
SS	Cheat	Stunt	4 Hole	Rush	Rush	Pursue	Rush
WS	Cheat	#2	Support	#2	#2	Bracket	#2
WC	#5	#5	Support	#5	#5	Bracket	#5

33. 43 Fire 4 Vs. 31 I Slot—Black Coverage (Diagram #256).

Diagram 256.

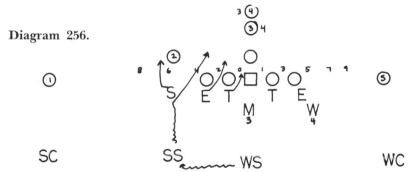

POS.	ALIGN.	KEY	RUN TO	PASS TO	ST. BACK	RUN AWAY	PASS AWAY
Sam	H	Stunt	6-8 Holes	Contain	Contain	Chase	Chase
SE	Heads	Fire	2 Hole	Rush	Rush	Pursue	Rush
ST	Heads	C	0 Hole	Rush	Rush	Pursue	Rush
Mike	Heads	#3	3-Free	#3	#3	Pursue	#3
WT	Heads	C	1 Hole	Rush	Rush	Pursue	Rush
WE	Switch	#5	7 Hole	Contain	Contain	Chase	Chase
Will	Switch	T-#4	5 Hole	Bakerman	Bakerman	Pursue	Bakerman

POS.	ALIGN.	KEY	RUN TO	PASS TO	ST. BACK	RUN AWAY	PASS AWAY
SC	#1	#1 Me	Support	#1	#1	Bracket	#1
SS	Cheat	Stunt	4 Hole	Rush	Rush	Pursue	Rush
WS	Cheat	#2	Support	#2	#2	Bracket	#2
WC	#5	#5 You	9 Hole	#5	#5	Bracket	#5

34. 43 Fire 4 Vs. 32 Flanker Split—Black Coverage (Diagram #257).

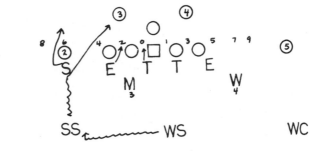

Diagram 257.

NOTE: Over Call.

POS.	ALIGN.	KEY	RUN TO	PASS TO	ST. BACK	RUN AWAY	PASS AWAY
Sam	H	Stunt	6-8 Holes	Contain	Contain	Chase	Chase
SE	Heads	Fire	2 Hole	Rush	Rush	Pursue	Rush
ST	Outside C	C	0 Hole	Rush	Rush	Pursue	Rush
Mike	Outside G	G-#3	Free	#3	#3	Pursue	Rush
WT	Heads	G	1-3 Holes	Rush	Rush	Pursue	Rush
WE	Outside	T-#4	5 Hole	Contain	Contain	Chase	Chase
Will	Regular	#4	7-9 Holes	#4	#4	Pursue	#4
SC	#1	#1 Me	Support	#1	#1	Bracket	#1
SS	Cheat	Stunt	4 Hole	Rush	Rush	Pursue	Rush
WS	Cheat	#2	Support	#2	#2	Bracket	#2
WC	#5	#5	Support	#5	#5	Bracket	#5

35. 43 Fire 4 Vs. 32 Trips—Check To Fire 3—See Number 20 this chapter.

36. 43 Fire 5 Vs. 22 Tight—Black Coverage (Diagram #258).

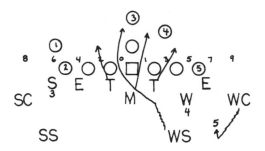

Diagram 258.

POS.	ALIGN.	KEY	RUN TO	PASS TO	ST. BACK	RUN AWAY	PASS AWAY
Sam	0	#2	6 Hole	#3	#3	Pursue	#3-Zone
SE	Outside	T	4 Hole	Contain	Contain	Chase	Chase
ST	Heads	Fire	2 Hole	Rush	Rush	Pursue	Rush
Mike	Heads	Fire	1 Hole	Rush	Rush	Pursue	Rush
WT	Heads	Fire	3 Hole	Rush	Rush	Pursue	Rush
WE	Switch	#5	7 Hole	Contain	Contain	Chase	Chase
Will	Switch	T-#4	5 Hole	Bakerman	Bakerman	Pursue	Bakerman
SC	See above	#1 You	8 Hole	Combo	Combo	Bracket	Combo
SS	See above	#2 You	Support	Combo	Combo	Bracket	Combo
WS	Cheat	Fire	0 Hole	Rush	Rush	Pursue	Rush
WC	See above	#5 You	9 Hole	#5	#5	Bracket	#5

37. 43 Fire 5 Vs. 22 Flanker Split—Black Coverage (Diagram #259).

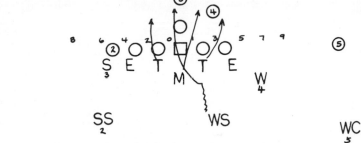

Diagram 259.

POS.	ALIGN.	KEY	RUN TO	PASS TO	ST. BACK	RUN AWAY	PASS AWAY
Sam	0	#2-#3	6 Hole	#3	#3	Pursue	#3
SE	Outside	T	4 Hole	Contain	Contain	Chase	Chase
ST	Heads	Fire	2 Hole	Rush	Rush	Pursue	Rush
Mike	Heads	Fire	1 Hole	Rush	Rush	Pursue	Rush
WT	Heads	Fire	3 Hole	Rush	Rush	Pursue	Rush
WE	Outside	T-4	5 Hole	Contain	Contain	Chase	Chase
Will	Regular	#4	7-9 Holes	Bakerman	Bakerman	Pursue	Bakerman
SC	#1	#1 Me	Support	#1	#1	Bracket	#1
SS	#2	#2 Me	8 Hole	#2	#2	Bracket	#2
WS	Cheat	Fire	0 Hole	Rush	Rush	Pursue	Rush
WC	#5	#5	Support	#5	#5	Bracket	#5

38. 43 Fire 5 Vs. 31 I Slot—Black Coverage (Diagram #260).

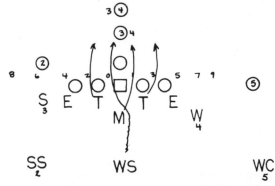

Diagram 260.

POS.	ALIGN.	KEY	RUN TO	PASS TO	ST. BACK	RUN AWAY	PASS AWAY
Sam	H	#2-#3	6 Hole	#3	#3	Pursue	#3
SE	Outside	T	4 Hole	Contain	Contain	Chase	Chase
ST	Heads	Fire	2 Hole	Rush	Rush	Pursue	Rush
Mike	Heads	Fire	1 Hole	Rush	Rush	Pursue	Rush
WT	Heads	Fire	3 Hole	Rush	Rush	Pursue	Rush
WE	Switch	#5	7 Hole	Contain	Contain	Chase	Chase
Will	Switch	T-4	5 Hole	Bakerman	Bakerman	Pursue	Bakerman
SC	#1	#1 Me	Support	#1	#1	Bracket	#1
SS	#2	#2 Me	8 Hole	#2	#2	Bracket	#2
WS	Cheat	Fire	0 Hole	Rush	Rush	Pursue	Rush
WC	#5	#5 You	9 Hole	#5	#5	Bracket	#5

39. 43 Fire 5 Vs. 32 Flanker Split—Black Coverage (Diagram #261).

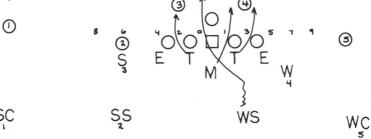

Diagram 261.

POS.	ALIGN.	KEY	RUN TO	PASS TO	ST. BACK	RUN AWAY	PASS AWAY
Sam	H	#2-#3	6 Hole	#3	#3	Pursue	#3
SE	Outside	T	4 Hole	Contain	Contain	Chase	Chase
ST	Heads	Fire	2 Hole	Rush	Rush	Pursue	Rush
Mike	Heads	Fire	1 Hole	Rush	Rush	Pursue	Rush
WT	Heads	Fire	3 Hole	Rush	Rush	Pursue	Rush
WE	Outside	T-4	5 Hole	Contain	Contain	Chase	Chase
Will	Regular	#4	7-9 Holes	Bakerman	Bakerman	Pursue	Bakerman

POS.	ALIGN.	KEY	RUN TO	PASS TO	ST. BACK	RUN AWAY	PASS AWAY
SC	#1	#1 Me	Support	#1	#1	Bracket	#1
SS	#2	#2 Me	8 Hole	#2	#2	Bracket	#2
WS	Cheat	Fire	0 Hole	Rush	Rush	Pursue	Rush
WC	#5	#5	Support	#5	#5	Bracket	#5

40. 43 Fire 5 Vs. 32 Trips—Black Coverage (Diagram #262).

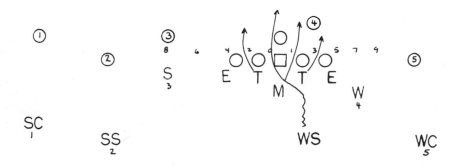

Diagram 262.

POS.	ALIGN.	KEY	RUN TO	PASS TO	ST. BACK	RUN AWAY	PASS AWAY
Sam	On #3	#3	6 Hole	#3	#3	Pursue	#3
SE	Outside	T	4 Hole	Contain	Contain	Chase	Chase
ST	Heads	Fire	2 Hole	Rush	Rush	Pursue	Rush
Mike	Heads	Fire	1 Hole	Rush	Rush	Pursue	Rush
WT	Heads	Fire	3 Hole	Rush	Rush	Pursue	Rush
WE	Outside	T-4	5 Hole	Contain	Contain	Chase	Chase
Will	Regular	#4	7-9 Holes	#4	#4	Pursue	#4
SC	On #1	#1 Me	Support	#1	#1	Bracket	#1
SS	On #2	#2 Me	8 Hole	#2	#2	Bracket	#2
WS	Cheat	Fire	0 Hole	Rush	Rush	Pursue	Rush
WC	On #5	#5	Support	#5	#5	Bracket	#5

41. 43 Fire 8 Vs. All Sets—Orange Coverage (Diagram #263).

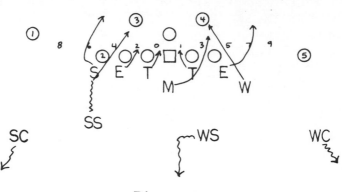

Diagram 263.

NOTE: This is an all out gambling blitz. It makes no difference what the set, shift or motion is. We go with it and pray.

POS.	ALIGN.	KEY	RUN TO	PASS TO	ST. BACK	RUN AWAY	PASS AWAY
Sam	0	Stunt	6-8 Holes	Contain	Contain	Chase	Chase
SE	Heads	Stunt	2 Hole	Rush	Rush	Pursue	Rush
ST	Heads	Stunt	0 Hole	Rush	Rush	Pursue	Rush
Mike	Heads	Stunt	3 Hole	Rush	Rush	Pursue	Rush
WT	Heads	Stunt	1 Hole	Rush	Rush	Pursue	Rush
WE	Outside	Stunt	7-9 Holes	Contain	Contain	Chase	Chase
Will	Regular	Stunt	5 Hole	Rush	Rush	Pursue	Rush
SC	On #1	Ball	Support	Deep 1/3	Deep 1/3	Bracket	Deep 1/3
SS	Cheat	Stunt	4 Hole	Rush	Rush	Pursue	Rush
WS	On #4	Ball	Support	Deep Mid	Deep Mid	Bracket	Deep Mid
WC	On #5	Ball	Support	Deep 1/3	Deep 1/3	Bracket	Deep 1/3

Adjustments

1. *Stunts.* At various times we mix in several stunts with our regular defenses. They can be used on both reading and pressing defenses. Since they usually only involve two players, we don't want

to make it a called defense. The procedure is to train the particular players to use these techniques at certain times or against certain offensive sets.

(a) *In and Out.* This really isn't a stunt but a technique used by Will and Weak End on every down. Will gives him an "in" call or an "out" call to establish hole responsibility in the advent of a run towards them. It also determines who forces the QB and who takes the pitch on option plays. When blitzes are called that involve Will, the same call is used only now Will fires on snap and is committed. See Diagram #264 and #265.

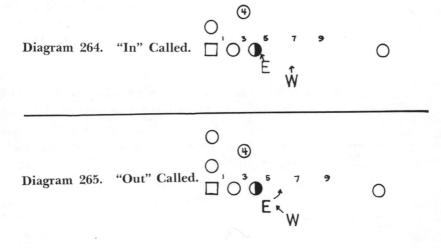

Diagram 264. "In" Called.

Diagram 265. "Out" Called.

(b) *TX.* This is old-fashioned terminology, but it has stayed with us down through the years. It is a cross charge between Sam and the Strong End. Sam always crosses first and we use this when blitzing on the strong side and are faced with an open side. Sam takes his SE responsibilities and his SE takes Sam's rules. See Diagram #266.

Diagram 266.

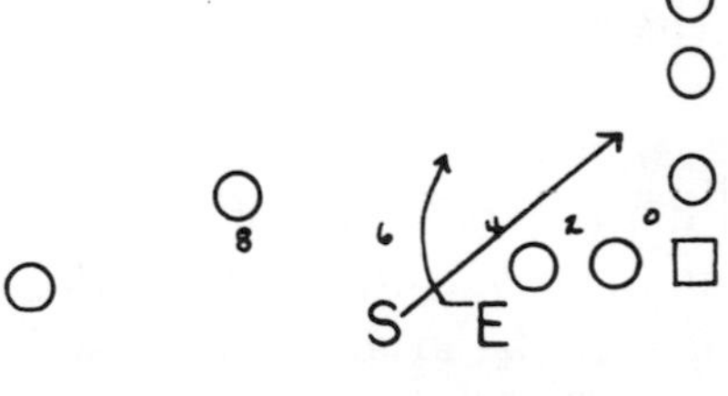

(c) *Invert TX.* This is basically the same stunt except on this one, the SE goes first. The best time to use this is when the offensive tight end flexes or splits only two or three yards. See Diagram #267.

(d) *Delay TX.* This stunt can be used by either outside line-backer and his end. We use this when blitzing to an open side and on sure passing downs. The technique here is to blitz straight ahead, drawing out the blocking pattern, and *then* executing a TX. See Diagram #268.

(e) *Switch.* This is an alignment adjustment more than a stunt. Its purpose is to get our end out wide enough to contain while our linebacker can concentrate on his pass assignment without worrying about having to contain. This is always done against a tight end when Will has to play a Bakerman. See Diagram #269.

(f) *Mike Fire.* This stunt frees Mike to fire his own. Sam knows when this is called that he has #3 man. Mike moves rapidly from side to side, in and out of the L.O.S. and tries to time his arrival, in either guard-tackle gap, just at the snap. He goes on and blitzes the gap. Our tackle on the side of Mike's blitz plays a 43 inside technique while the other tackle plays a "Spy" technique. See Diagram #270.

(g) *Twist.* This is a stunt, or cross charge, between our end and our tackle on either side. On occasions we have had a twist on both sides at once. Its purpose is pass rush, and should be called on passing downs. Our end aligns a little further off of the L.O.S. Our tackle takes all the ball he can and drives through the offensive guards outside shoulder. Our end steps behind his tackles charge and blitzes the guard-center tap. See Diagram #271.

(h) *Tango.* This is a cross charge executed by our two tackles. Our Weak Tackle crosses first and must get to the "0" hole, or strong center-guard gap. The Strong Tackle steps behind and charges the opposite center-guard gap. Again, this is a stunt that is used primarily as a pass rush. See Diagram #272.

2. *Field Position Adjustments.* So far in this book we have not covered this vital area of pass defense. It is the hardest part of coaching pass defense, and it is the hardest for the players to learn. Players must be made aware of where they are on the field of play. Sidelines must be used by the defense. Wide sides must be played

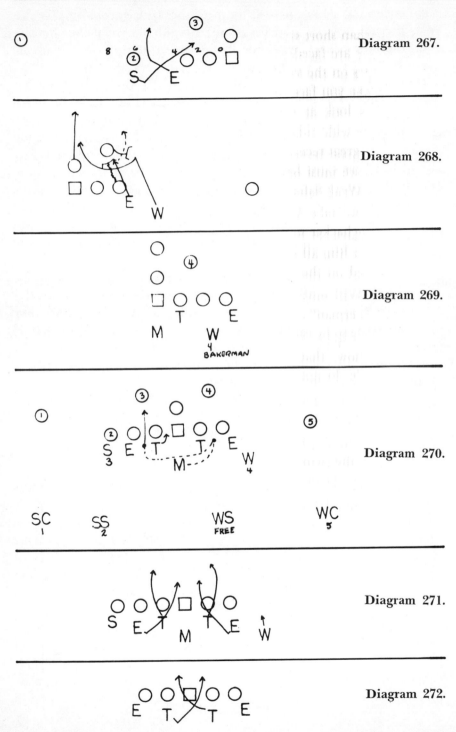

Diagram 267.

Diagram 268.

Diagram 269.

Diagram 270.

Diagram 271.

Diagram 272.

differently than short sides. As an example, let's consider Blue Coverage and we are faced with a team that uses twins. Twins are two wide eligibles on the same side. People who use this, do so because they can make you face their two best receivers on one side.

First, let's look at the situation where the opponent puts his Twins to the wide side of the field. The ball is on the hash. Here we have two great receivers and all that room for them to maneuver. Defensively, we must help our Strong Corner and Strong Safety by moving our Weak Safety over to where he can back them up. When we do this, we take Weak Safety help away from the weak side. Our Will linebacker must now play Bakerman on #4 which means he must cover him all the way without help. Most always there will be a tight end on the weak side when there are wide twins to the strong side. Will must now call a "Switch" with his end as he has gotten a "Bakerman" call from our Weak Safety. This enables him to get off the line so he can cover #4. See Diagram #273.

Suppose, now, that our opponents align their twins *into* the boundary. We do not have as big a problem with them now that their maneuver room has been reduced. However, Will has a tougher run problem with a tight weak end into the field. Also our Weak Safety can now help to the field and still not be completely out of support to the twins side. We do not call "Bakerman," our Weak Safety does not favor the twins side, and we remain sound to the field. See Diagram #274.

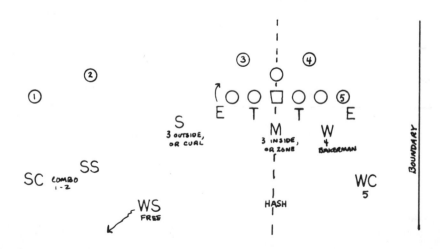

Diagram 273.

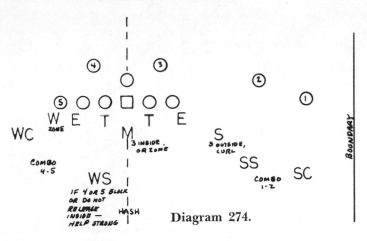

Diagram 274.

Next, consider zone or jump coverage when field position is involved. Zones change according to position of the ball. It is very well to simply tell the four short zone men that they each have one fourth of the field up to ten yards. Also it is simple if each one of the three deep knows he has the deep one third of the field. This is true if the ball is exactly in the middle of the field. But the ball isn't always in the middle. At least 60% of the time the ball is on one hash mark or the other. Due to the fact that we might be jumping a good receiver who is lined up into the side line with the ball on that hash mark, we have created one heck of a long flat to the wide side. The following diagrams will show that our perimeter people have many various places to sprint to in order to get into their zones (Diagrams #275-#280).

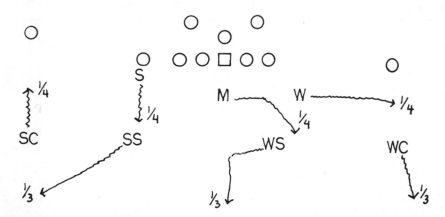

Diagram 275. Strong Jump—Middle of the Field.

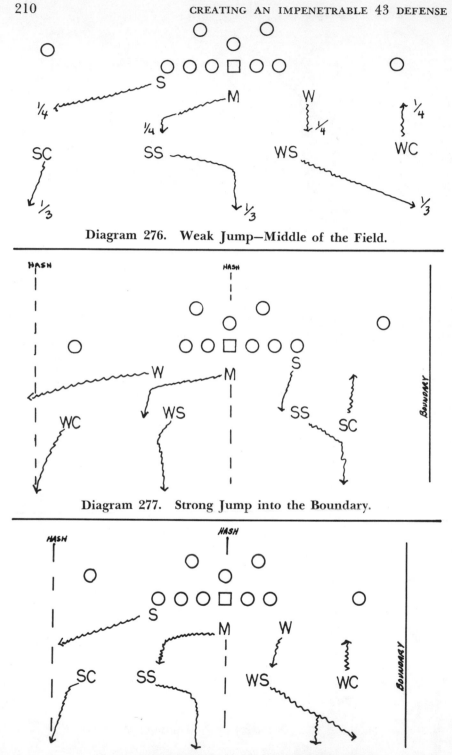

Diagram 276.   Weak Jump—Middle of the Field.

Diagram 277.   Strong Jump into the Boundary.

Diagram 278.   Weak Jump into the Boundary.

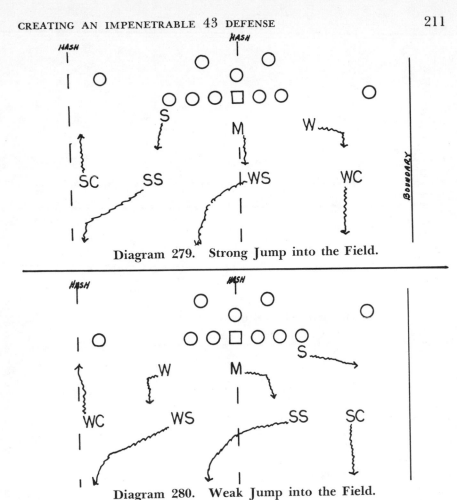

Diagram 279.   Strong Jump into the Field.

Diagram 280.   Weak Jump into the Field.

This will give you an idea of why so much time must be spent in perimeter drill. All of these situations must be covered over and over again. It also explains why practice movies must be taken. One secondary coach just can't watch every player's alignment in relation to formation as well as field position.

Outside linebackers must always be aware of field position, as well as formation, on their original alignments. When Sam or Will has the sideline his side, he can always play tighter into the formation. Also he can play closer into the ball when the threat of the quick outside is not present. An example of this would be against an I formation (Diagrams #281-#283).

3. *Special Play Adjustments.*

A. *Triple Option.*

Diagram 281.   Will Versus an Open I Formation.

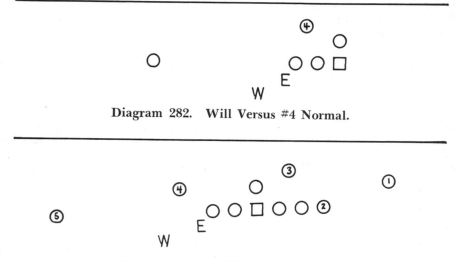

Diagram 282.   Will Versus #4 Normal.

Diagram 283.   Will Versus #4 Wide.

This segment could be endless, but as an example, I will show here how we adjusted our 4-3 to the triple option offense.

We called this adjustment 43 Mike Strong and most of it was charted previously in this chapter. However, we had to add a couple of things to it. The toughest thing the triple option people were doing was to release their tight end off and hitting him quick with a short pass anytime your Strong Safety came up to support. This means we had to defense them without support of our Strong Corner or Strong Safety. We still had to have somebody for the veer man, somebody for the QB, and somebody for the pitchman. We lined Mike up in front of their offensive tackle. Our Strong End pinched in tough and took the veer man, whether he had the ball or not. Mike then "scraped off" on flow to, and took the QB. Sam flattened out the tight end release, and was in position to take the pitch.

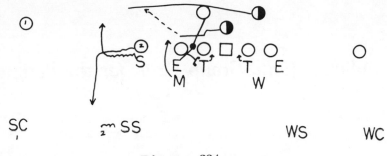

Diagram 284.

Our tackles played a 43 inside technique and Will had to favor strong. The same offense to the weak side was not as tough because of their split weak end which allowed Weak Saftey support. Here is how it looks diagramed (Diagram #284).

This was one of our better plans. One year we opened with Houston and shut their triple option off completely. They shifted gears and hurt us with their throwing game and that very good weak lead draw, but we upset them because they didn't kill us with the triple option.

9

Individual and Group Drills for the Perimeter

1. WARM UP DRILLS

We have noticed that defensive perimeter people seem to have a tendency to pulled groin muscles. It figures because of the very nature of their type play. They must run backwards and change directions quickly. They react on another's actions. This quick change of body position can easily result in muscle damage high in the leg. Such things as groins, ham strings, and thigh pulls are not uncommon; in fact, these injuries far outnumber other types. To counteract this problem we instigated a special warm up drill for defensive backs and linebackers. We called this Hell drill. The drills really aren't that bad, but it was a short catchy name. We started practice every day with Hell drill, and it never took more than ten minutes. Following is our Hell drill:

A. Stretching

1. *Rocking Chair.* Players sit on the ground with knee under chins. They grasp around their legs and rock backwards on their spines.

2. *Bicycle.* From the sitting position players go into bicycle position. After a few short "pumps" of their legs, they "scissors" their legs, making sure to stretch the groin. Finally, they roll over farther and touch the ground with their toes behind their head.

3. *Neck Bridges.* Still on the ground, the players come to the back supine position and arch up on head and feet. After rocking back and forth, they do a couple of flip overs both forward and backwards.

214

4. *Mountain Climber.* Back in the standing position, players step out forward with one leg as far as they can stretch and hug the thigh of the outstretched leg. This is repeated with both legs several times.

5. *Trunk Rotation.* Hands on hips and roll out the mid-section both ways.

6. *Ham Strings.* From the standing position players cross one leg over the other and then touch toes. Cross the other leg over and repeat.

7. *Groin Stretcher.* Players stand with legs split apart as far as possible and then try to touch the ground with their elbows.

8. *Chase the Bunny.* From the forward leaning rest position players bring alternate legs up and back.

B. Striding

1. *Long Strides.* Players run across the field taking exaggerated strides.

2. *Cross Overs.* Same as above only the long exaggerated strides are cross overs.

C. Agility

These drills were described in Chapter 2, so I'll just name them here:

1. Quick around
2. Dizzy Izzy
3. Grape vine run
4. Switch run
5. Zig Zag run
6. Wave drills
7. Rope runs

D. Isometrics

We have a long shiver board attached to metal poles, and we use it for three things: Shiver Isometrics, Neck Isometrics and Shuffle & Shiver.

E. Quick Quicks

We always ended this drill with Quick Quicks so we could start practice on an enthusiastic note. We always did three or four of the standard ones. Such as Toe Tapper, Side Straddle, Wayback and Quarter Eagle.

2. STANCE AND ALIGNMENTS

Our secondary players used pretty much the same stance as our linebackers. Really, the best way to describe it would be to say that it is similar to a basketball player's position on defense. In general the outside foot is back. This is true until position is near the boundary, then of course the inside foot can be back. There will be some occasions when playing a man head up where the feet should be parallel.

Alignments depend on the defense called, field position and the formation of the offense. Alignment drills consist mainly of having an offensive skeleton of ends and backs take various formations from hash to hash and simply having your secondary align correctly each time. Here are some general rules.

Corners

Versus tight sets you are the force man and will be playing Combo. This is a "You" call. In general, you are three yards outside and three yards deep off of the widest opponent. Against wideout receivers you have your outside foot back and shade the receiver to his outside. As a general rule we want everything to happen "inside" of our perimeter. However, Corners never get closer to the sideline than seven or eight yards. Depth off of the wideout is eight to ten yards. This will be a "Me" call and you do not have immediate support so you can be a bit deeper. Against twins, where there are two wideouts close together, on the same side, you align on the widest one. Since your safety will be out on the next inside eligible, you must align the same distance off of your man as he is off of his. This prevents you both aligning on the same plane as the receivers are not on the same plane. If the defense called is Zone, your depth increases a yard or so, but we don't want to tip off Zone.

Safeties

The Strong Safety versus a tight set is just outside Sam at a depth of seven or eight yards. When the offense has one wide out your side, you are in the same spot a yard or so deeper unless the tight end flexes, then you play him head up. Sam may have a "Him" call, in which case you align inside of Sam. These alignments are based on support. The Weak Safety aligns on the same plane as the Strong Safety just outside of the number four back in the offensive backfield. If #4 is in an I, goes in motion, or is aligned behind center, then the Weak Safety aligns over the center.

3. AGILITY

These drills have been described in Chapter 2. We do place a lot of emphasis on backward running drills for defensive backs.

4. TACKLING

Our defensive backs do all the tackling drills described in Chapter 2. It might be interesting to repeat here that our backs work against our offensive wide receivers in Hamburger drill. They are forced to shed blockers and tackle, just like anyone else on defense.

5. BREAK ON THE BALL DRILLS

a. Back Reaction Drill

Defensive backs align in front of a passer one at a time. On signal they back pedal straight back. The passer throws the ball rather hard over the defender's head or just to either side high. Defender catches the ball at the highest point he possibly can. He puts it away and sprints back up field with it. He should always holler "Oskie" to develop the habit (Diagram #285).

b. Forward Reaction Drill

This is just the reverse of the above drill. The players align 20 yards deep in front the passer. They run towards the passer one at a time. The passer throws the ball over the defenders head forcing him to break stride and reach for the ball (Diagram #286).

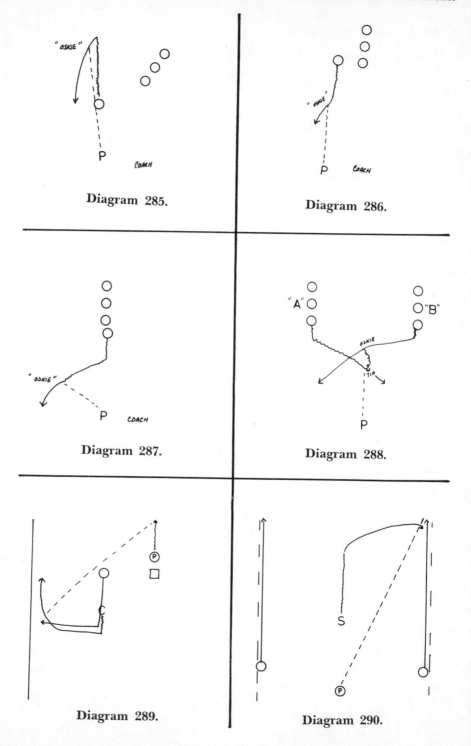

Diagram 285.

Diagram 286.

Diagram 287.

Diagram 288.

Diagram 289.

Diagram 290.

c. Angle Intercept Drill

This is the same as the forward drill except that the defender breaks off his forward run at 10 yards and takes an angle away from the passer. The passer then throws a lead pass for interception (Diagram #287).

d. Tip Drill

There are many ways to do tip drills, but the best for secondary men is the one that has two lines (players in tandem) 20 yards from the passer. Player in line A runs across in front of passer and "tips" the pass. Player in line B starts a bit later and paces himself behind the crossing player from line A. He must react to the tipped ball and catch it. Players then switch lines (Diagram #288).

e. Sideline Gauge Drill

An offensive end executes a sideline cut. Make defender wait until end is two steps from him. He then shuffles back and out. Make passer "hang" the ball to the outside. The defender plays the ball and takes it away from the end. This is lapping with the sideline (Diagram #289).

f. Hash Mark Deep Drill

Put two receivers, one on each hash mark. Place the defender in the middle of the field at a depth of 12 yards. On signal both ends sprint straight down their hash mark. The defender should turn and sprint straight back. Passer should throw the ball when receivers have covered 15 yards. The defender should turn his back and go for the interception point if the ball is thrown to the receiver to his back or sprint directly to the interception point if the ball is thrown to the side he is facing (Diagram #290).

g. Lateral Reaction

This drill can be done with any number of defenders and receivers. If the teaching emphasis is on one secondary man, place him at a distance of 25 yards from the passer. Station two receivers in a static position on either side of the defender. The idea is to

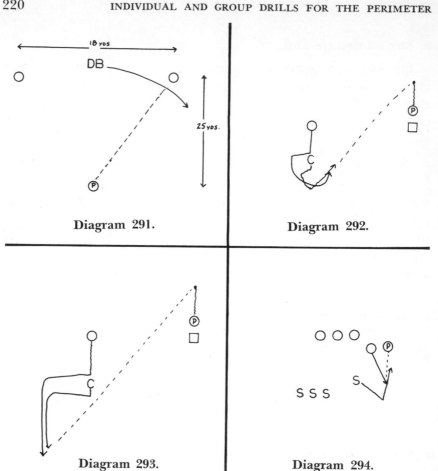

Diagram 291.

Diagram 292.

Diagram 293.

Diagram 294.

throw the ball to either one of the two stationary receivers. The defender, in the middle, breaks on the ball and goes for the interception. When you first start this drill the receivers should only be six yards away from the defender. This builds confidence. Gradually, the distance is increased. We figure a good defender can cover nine yards in either direction at this depth. This means one defender can actually cover 18 yards laterally. Theoretically then, three defenders can lap the entire width of the field (Diagram #291).

6. ONE ON ONE DRILLS

Since our basic coverage is Blue, we will be playing a lot of man to man coverage. Therefore, it is necessary that we work on one on one situations a lot.

a. One on One Games

All we need here is a passer, several receivers and one defender. The receivers run any goofy short route they can think of to get themselves open. The passer simply waits until he can throw. Of course, the advantage here is with the offense so it is best to use B team receivers (Diagram #292).

b. One on One Routes

The defender aligns on his man. On the snap the QB and receiver run pre-called routes. The defender runs backward keeping his eyes on the receiver. This is where the defender learns how much cushion he can allow. He must react on the receivers breaks. Everyone in the drill hollers "Ball" when the passer releases it. On deep routes the defender must watch the receiver's eyes to alert him to the fact that the ball is in the air. This physical skill is most important. It is not easy to run hip to hip with a fast man and know at just what point you must find the football. One of the biggest errors in one on one coverage is to take your eyes off the receiver, even for a split second (Diagram #293).

c. Dog Fight Drill

Run short straight routes at a defender where the ball and receiver are in the same line of sight. The defender gets position on the receiver and "plays through" the receiver to get to the ball (Diagram #294).

d. Free Safety Drill

This drill is similar to the hash mark drill except that the two wide receivers each have a cornerback covering them one on one. The Free Safety retreats staying as deep as the deepest receiver and then breaks on the ball to help his corner (Diagram #295).

e. Free Safety Choice Drill

This is a formation recognition drill. The Free Safety knows if #4 and #5 release weak he must support that side first. If only #5

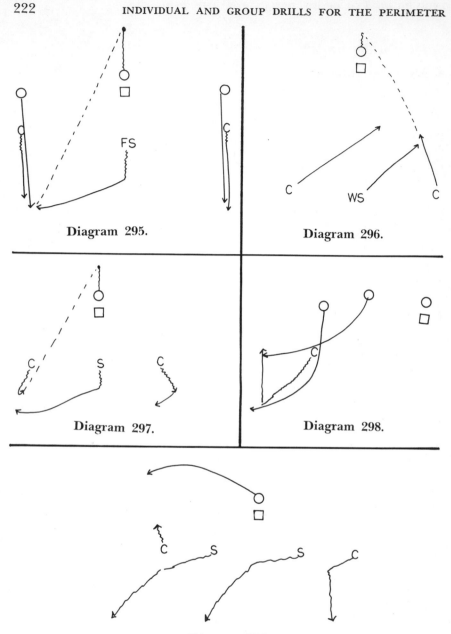

Diagram 295.

Diagram 296.

Diagram 297.

Diagram 298.

Diagram 299.

releases weak, then he can support strong. He also knows if the offense has three receivers strong, two of which are wide, he must call "Bakerman" and support the flood side. This drill then places him in these various situations.

7. ZONE DRILLS

a. Deep Forward Drill

Place the Free Safety and two corners downfield about 50 yards. The passer throws, intentionally, a 30 yard pass. The three defenders come forward fast and judge the ball for a catch at its highest point. Deep men get the feel of the ball as they come forward full speed (Diagram #296).

b. Deep Backward Drill

This is the same idea as the deep forward drill, except the three deep get the practice of going for deep passes.

c. Overlap Drill

The three deep men take normal positions. On the snap they start back into their zone positions. This is where they can cover their ⅓'s and still overlap one another. Passer throws to various spots in these zones. If the left corner calls for the ball, the safety is always covering him up—that is, he gets behind him. If the safety calls for the ball, the nearest corner backs him up. Also the ball should be thrown outside the corners who are lapping with the boundary (Diagram #297).

d. Two in One Zone Drill

Two receivers, such as an end and halfback run a flood into the corner's zone. The corner keeps depth and width on the deepest receiver and then comes up fast if the ball is thrown to the short man. The more width the halfback keeps, the better position he is in to cover both receivers (Diagram #298).

e. Sliding Zones Drill

Zones change according to field position, and or movement of the ball. This drill is similar to the one used to coach linebackers to know where their zones are (Diagram #299).

f. Confidence Drill

Place two wide-out receivers against a full perimeter. Also declare that six more "ends" will be eligible. All eight of these men run any route they want to. By getting the defenders into their proper zones they should be able to break up the pass no matter how many receivers go out for a pass (Diagram #300).

8. DOUBLE COVER DRILLS

These are really zone drills, but are a little more specialized. The two positions most affected are Strong Safety and Will. There are many ways these two players can play their short zones. Basically what we want is harassment of the wide-out, taking away what is most dangerous according to the situation, and finally playing the zone which means the possibility of other receivers in that zone. This is zone double coverage. We also have doubles off Blue Coverage, which means we are going to play one receiver short and deep, or inside-outside. As you can see the two techniques are entirely different. On Blue double we want the short man to play the receiver as tight as possible without regard for other receivers who might come into that zone. We must prevent the short pass to the good receiver. When the receiver finally loses our short man, then our deep man picks him up. Due to time left in the game, however, zone doubles may become like Blue doubles. Here we must prevent the sideline cut to stop the clock, so we don't care if a second receiver comes short into that zone. We want short completions in the field of play. Also if there is only time for one or two plays, our emphasis now shifts to our short man simply keeping the wide receiver from getting deep at all. These drills then consist of working with one short and one deep defender playing a wide receiver in different situations. Have two sets going at once (Diagram #301).

9. BUMP AND RUN DRILLS

We used the same set up as above. A corner versus a wide out and a passer. The idea here is to jump up on the wide receiver just before snap and knock him off stride and then simply run with him. This can be done because, in theory, the two have at least an even

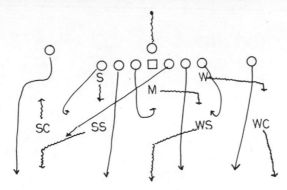

Diagram 300.

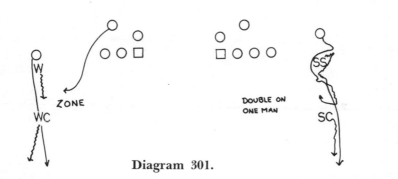

Diagram 301.

start. It also can get you beat in a hurry if your man isn't a real good athlete. We did this occasionally as a surprise, but most of the time when we jumped up on somebody, we also had someone backing us up deep. Our jump coverage and Gray coverage uses this technique. Practice on this drill should determine if your corners are capable of Bump and Run coverage without help.

10. SUPPORT DRILLS

Outside Run Drill

Place two dummies where our ends should be. Use the whole perimeter, four backs and three linebackers versus a skeleton offensive backfield and tight end. The offense runs outside running plays with an occasional running pass. Defensively we want to work on our support calls of "You, Me and Him." See Diagram #302.

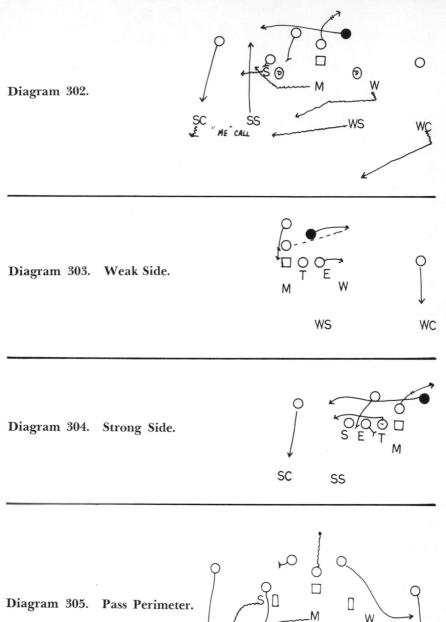

Diagram 302.

Diagram 303.   Weak Side.

Diagram 304.   Strong Side.

Diagram 305.   Pass Perimeter.

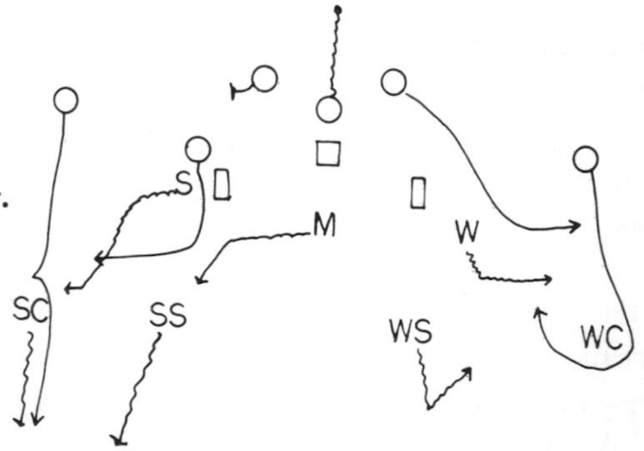

Diagram 306. Run Defense.

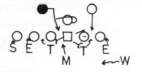

11. HALF LINE DRILLS

This is simply what it says. The offense has a center, one half a line, and back field. Defensively we will have the Weak Safety, Weak Corner, Will and Mike linebackers, one End and one tackle working against the half offense that works on its weak side attack. At the same time one half an offense, working on strong side plays, goes against our strong side people. See Diagrams #303 and #304.

12. PERIMETER DRILL

This is our main drill once the season is underway. We spend at least forty minutes a day on perimeter. In the middle of the field we have an offensive set of backs and receivers working against all our defensive backs with one set of linebackers. Away and behind the passing offense we have a full offensive team working against all of our line men with the other set of linebackers. Against our perimeter we are working mostly pass offense; against our line we run mostly run plays. At half the period we swap the linebackers. See Diagrams #305 and #306.

13. PURSUIT AND OSKIE DRILL

We always ran these two drills at the same time. They are good teaching drills but require a lot of running so we used them as conditioning drills as well. These drills are run back to back. The pursuit drill uses all eleven defensive men. They face seven down linemen and four or five backs who run wide one at a time. Dummies are placed on the line of scrimmage about five yards from each boundary. When the starting signal is given, the one back with the ball runs wide, turning up field between the bag and the boundary. Force men tag him behind the line. The on-side line-backer tags him next, using an inside-out approach. The rest of the defense uses correct pursuit angles and tag him progressively as he runs up field. As soon as they tag, they hustle back and get lined up, because the next back is ready to go the other way (Diagram #307).

While this is going on the second defensive unit is facing just a

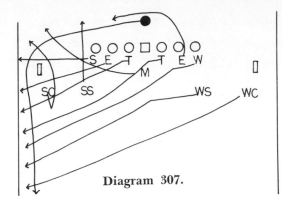

Diagram 307.

passer. As the passer sets up, the linemen rush him and the perimeter gets into their zones. The passer throws an intentional interception. Everyone breaks on the ball and then leads the ball carrier. At the end they throw a roll block at the ground. Quickly they line up and do it again. Defensive units swap after four or five minutes (Diagram #308).

50 DEFENSIVE DO'S AND DON'TS

1. Don't line up further apart than 2 paces on the LOS.
2. Do earn a tie with the blocker, then escape and pursue.
3. Don't hit blocker head on, hit either shoulder.
4. Do stay square with the LOS.
5. Don't let blocker into your "strike" zone.
6. Do deliver a blow.
7. Don't run around pressure.
8. Do keep leverage on the blocker and the ball.
9. Don't leave your feet when tackling.
10. Do retreat through your position if you are forced to retreat.
11. Don't tackle with your head behind the ball carrier.
12. Do pursue on an interception angle while preventing cut backs.
13. Don't run the "inside arc."
14. Do rush the passer in lanes.
15. Don't jump off the ground before passer releases the ball.
16. Do keep hands and arms up when pass is imminent.
17. Don't let pass blockers get into your body—Keep them at arms length.
18. Do keep outside edge on all blockers if you are a container.
19. Don't tackle low in an open field.
20. Do play further off the ball if you are having trouble with keying.
21. Don't hit a big man high.
22. Do aim where they bend when tackling.

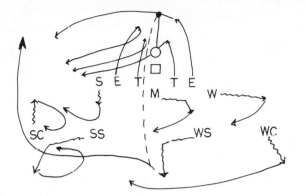

Diagram 308.

23. Do keep your head between the ball carrier and the goal line.
24. Don't try to get to POA without insuring your assignment.
25. Do keep your outside leg free.
26. Don't get driven off the line—make a pile if necessary.
27. Do drive blockers into POA on short yards.
28. Don't aim for the kicker on punts, field goal and extra point attempts.
29. Do develop a smell for screen and draw.
30. Don't ever line up closer to the sideline than 8 yards.
31. Do holler "Screen and draw" at the appropriate times.
32. Don't ever think you are out of a screen or draw. Take a new angle.
33. Do always know how many yards your team can safely give up.
34. Don't become half rusher, half defender.
35. Do key from the inside out if not hit on the snap.
36. Don't butt a down runner. Go over the top.
37. Do lower your stance the closer you align to the ball.
38. Don't watch backfield action.
39. Do go for interceptions at the highest point of the trajectory that you can get to.
40. Don't walk or trot when coming off the field—sprint.
41. Do anticipate the offense but don't guess.
42. Don't cross the center fast if you are the off linebacker.
43. Do bounce in place if you aren't sure of the POA.
44. Don't converse across the line. This ain't no party.
45. Do huddle quickly.
46. Don't get offside, ever, if the distance to go is less than 5 yards.
47. Do break on all thrown balls, no matter where you are.
48. Don't take blame or credit for the big plays.
49. Do know where the ball is according to the boundary.
50. Don't get provoked into a fight.

Part III

THE GOAL LINE DEFENSE

10

Coaching the Goal Line—Long Yards

The game of football today is not only more wide open, but is longer in duration than it was just a few years ago. Due to rule changes, each team in a game will average about fifteen more plays than they did just a few short years ago. It is not uncommon to be on defense 85 plays a game. When you add to this the rapid development of high school passers and receivers, you can easily see that you are going to be in your goal line defense frequently. So, sooner or later, the balance of victory or defeat will rest on how well you can play defense in the goal line area. Just about anybody can get to your goal line area nowadays, but when they get there, it is a whole new ball game. This is the only place on the field of play that the defense really has the advantage.

I came to these conclusions a couple of years back, and we began to spend a great deal more practice time on goal line defense. We also spent a great deal of staff time in planning on this phase of the game. Gradually, we got better and with that came confidence; a necessary ingredient for any line stand. You can never divorce morale from football, but on the goal line it becomes paramount. In a recent season, we executed 19 successful goal line stands. We not only stopped our opponent from scoring a touchdown but also prevented a field goal. This had to be the deciding factor in our 9-1-1 season.

The first thing we had to do in studying goal line defense was to properly define just where the goal line areas were and how to defend each. The first area would have to be goal line normal. Any time we are forced to hold the offense to two yards or less per try we considered ourselves to be in a goal line normal situation. By multiplying the downs remaining by two we could quickly tell if the situation were normal or not. For instance, first down and eight or less is normal. Also, second down and six or less, third down and four or less, and fourth down and two are all normal goal line situations. By normal, then, we mean that our defense must be capable of limiting the offense to a two yards or less gain. By doing this we create a goal line long situation. When we have this condition, we felt we could now use a different defense, because our "cushion" was better and the offense must now shift gears and call a different type offense. Long situations, therefore, are, first and nine or more, second and seven or more, third and five or more, and fourth and three or more. Naturally, a two point conversion is the same as fourth and three and is a long situation. The last area of goal line defense is goal line short. Regardless of the down, when our opponent has two or less yards to go for a touchdown, we are in a goal line short situation. We felt that this area must be defended differently than goal line normal.

The next three chapters of this book will cover these three goal line situations.

GOAL LINE LONG

Starting from the outside in, this chapter will deal with the goal line long areas. We called this defense 61. The aims of this defense were:

a. Carry over from what we played elsewhere on the field.

b. Sound run defense, but not heavy penetration. Pursuit now becomes important.

c. Containment by our outside linebackers.

d. Tight man coverage, when possible, knowing we did not have to defend in depth.

e. 61 defense, then, is similar to 43 Fire 1. As such, all rules versus all sets, and all motions are the same as we would play up field.

1. 61 versus a 22 tight (Diagram #309).

Sam   Align and key the same as 43 Fire 1. Place more emphasis on containment of sprint-outs and running passes than when you were in other areas of the field. Poor containment down here is fatal.

S.E.   Same as 43 Fire 1.

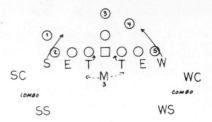

Diagram 309.

S.T. Same as 43 Inside. Mike can give you the 0 or 2 holes for a quick charge. He simply will call your name. If he calls other tackles name then you execute a "spy" technique.

Mike Align and key the same as 43 Inside, but since this is the same as Fire 1, you have #3 man. This means you will have to call an "over" if #3 is in a strong half-back position.

W.T. Same as S.T.

W.E. Same as S.E.

Will Same as Sam.

S.C. Combo with S.S.

S.S. Combo with S.C.

W.S. Combo with W.C.

W.C. Combo with W.S.

2. 61 versus a 22 Flanker Split (Diagram #310).

Sam Same as 43 Fire 1. Be alert for "him" call from your Strong Safety.

S.E. Same as 43 Fire 1.

S.T. Same as versus 22 tight.

Mike Same as versus 22 tight.

W.T. Same as versus 22 tight.

W.E. Same as 43 Fire 1.

Will Same as Sam.

S.C. #1 "Me" call.

S.S. #2 "Me" call.

W.S. #4 "Me" call.

W.C. #5 "Me" call.

Diagram 310.

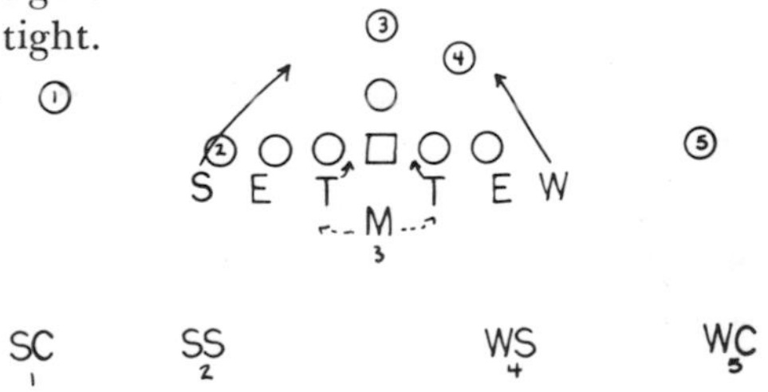

3. 61 versus 31 I Slot (Diagram #311).

Sam TX with your end.

S.E. TX with Sam.

S.T. Same as versus 22 tight.

Mike Same as versus 22 tight.

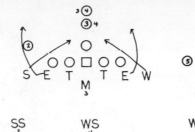

Diagram 311.

W.T.	Same as versus 22 tight.
Will	Same as versus 22 tight.
S.C.	#1 Me call.
S.S.	#2 Me call.
W.S.	Align over center. Play Combo with W.C. if flow is weak, or if #4 releases weak. Anything else back up your S.C. and S.S. on #1 and #2.
W.C.	Play Combo with W.S. if flow is weak or if #4 releases weak, if not play #5 man.

4. 61 versus 32 Flanker Split (Diagram #312).

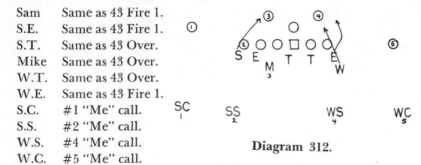

Diagram 312.

Sam	Same as 43 Fire 1.
S.E.	Same as 43 Fire 1.
S.T.	Same as 43 Over.
Mike	Same as 43 Over.
W.T.	Same as 43 Over.
W.E.	Same as 43 Fire 1.
S.C.	#1 "Me" call.
S.S.	#2 "Me" call.
W.S.	#4 "Me" call.
W.C.	#5 "Me" call.

5. 61 versus 31 Strong Twins (Diagram #313).

Sam	Come hard outside—No TX on an "over" call.
S.E.	Play offensive tackle almost head up.
S.T.	Same as 43 Over.
Mike	Same as 43 Over. Use Fire 1 rules #3 man.
W.T.	Same as 43 Fire 1.
S.C.	Play Combo with S.S. on #1 and #2—"You" call.
S.S.	Play Combo with S.S. on #1 and #2—"You" call.
W.S.	Align over center, be ready to back up on #1 and #2 if #4 doesn't release. Weak screen is dangerous here. Be sure #4 does not become a receiver.
W.C.	#5 man.

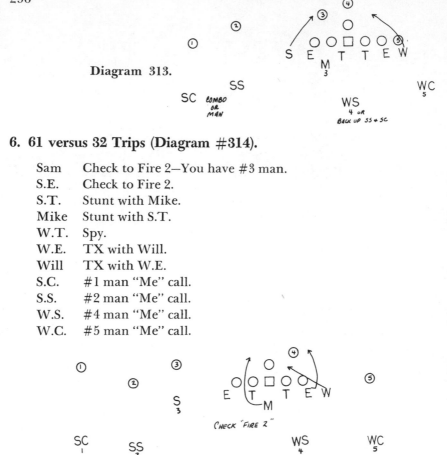

Diagram 313.

6. 61 versus 32 Trips (Diagram #314).

Sam   Check to Fire 2—You have #3 man.
S.E.   Check to Fire 2.
S.T.   Stunt with Mike.
Mike   Stunt with S.T.
W.T.   Spy.
W.E.   TX with Will.
Will   TX with W.E.
S.C.   #1 man "Me" call.
S.S.   #2 man "Me" call.
W.S.   #4 man "Me" call.
W.C.   #5 man "Me" call.

Diagram 314.

This covers a variety of sets against a 61 defense. As you can see this defense is not unlike 43 Fire 1. The main difference is mental. Sam and Will know they must contain. Inside people know that pass rush and pursuit is important. Secondary people know they can cover tighter.

Coaching the Goal Line—Normal Yards

Goal line "long" didn't change a great deal from our up field rules and techniques. Goal line normal is different in rules and techniques. Wherever we can, we will keep the same terminology and carry over what we can, but this is a whole new ball game. We called this defense 65. Our aims and philosophies are as follows:

a. Tough hard penetration. We must give up some pursuit versus the run.

b. We must contain the running game to less than two yards per try.

c. Whenever possible we will achieve a double stack with our Mike linebacker and Weak Safety aligned behind (or almost behind) our defensive tackles.

d. Our secondary will seek to stay away from zone, but will still have to Combo, Banjo, and Sambo close receivers.

e. Secondary people never align deeper than three yards off the ball.

1. 65 versus 22 Tight (Diagram #315).

Sam   Align in a three point stance with your inside ear even with tight end's outside ear. Come hard on the snap through the tight end's outside knee. You must react to end's block, but not at the price of reducing your charge. If he tries to release, you should knock him off stride. Don't get hooked. Your hole responsibility is 6, but you must limit hole 4. Against certain teams our Strong Safety will give you the 4 hole and take the 6 hole himself, but it depends on who you are playing. If you

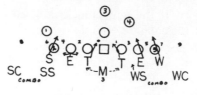

Diagram 315.

aren't blocked on the LOS, use progressive inside out keys. Stay as deep as the ball and contain. Chase—contain plays away. Remember this, it is most important. Force the option play as quickly as possible. This is different from up field. We want this developed right now.

S.E.   Align ear and ear on the offensive tackle and use a four point stance. Charge his outside knee and take the 4 hole responsibility. There is one exception and that applies to the set diagramed above. You are faced with what we call the ghost. (Ghost means there is no halfback lined up on your side.) When this happens, you aren't faced with the quick shot. Align head up the offensive tackle, and play him square taking both the 2 and 4 holes. On this kind of set you are more apt to meet traps, counters and sweeps, all of which you can play better if you don't penetrate.

S.T.   Align head on the offensive guard using a low four point stance. Charge his inside knee and take the 0 hole. Secure the sneak. Drive for penetration.

Mike   Align head up center just outside of your tackle's feet. This is one of the sets you cannot stack against. Key #3 and take the 2 and 3 hole responsibility first. On pass show you will play #3 man. You can cover #3 from where you are and your Strong Safety must play Combo with his Strong Corner on #1 and #2.

W.T.   Same as S.T. (take 1 hole).

W.E.   Same as S.E. (take 5 hole).

Will   Same as Sam (take 7 hole but limit the 5 hole).

S.C.   Align two yards deep and two yards wider than the close wing. Play Combo with your Strong Safety on #1 and #2. Key the #1 man. If he blocks, support right now, you are the forceman. Take the 8 hole responsibility.

S.S.   Align behind Sam. If you give him the 4 hole, then you have the 6 hole, or vice versa. If not, you support Sam in both. Key the tight end and wing back. You are playing Combo with your S.C. Both must block before you support. If the wing blocks and end releases, you must cover the end (#2) man for man.

W.S.   Align just outside #4. Key #4 and help in the 3 hole first if #4 blocks straight away. If not keep leverage on the ball. Play a Combo with your W.C. on #4 and #5.

W.C.   Align two yards deep and two yards outside #5. Key #4 and #5. You are playing a Combo on them with your W.S. If either #4 or #5 release outside, you must cover the one that releases. If both block, you can support and take the 9 hole.

2. 65 versus 22 Flanker Split (Diagram #316).

Front 7   Same as versus 22 Tight.
S.C.   #1 man "Me" call.
S.S.   #2 man "Me" call.
W.S.   #4 man "Me" call.
W.C.   #5 man "Me" call.

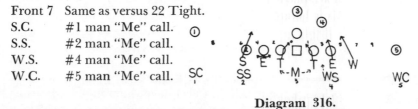

Diagram 316.

3. 65 versus 31 I Slot (Diagram #317).

Sam   Align on slot man up to a width of four yards. Play him exactly as if he were a tight end. As soon as his width gets more than four or five feet, you can beat him back to the inside. All 65 rules previously described apply.

S.E.   Same as versus 22 Tight.

S.T.   Same as versus 22 Tight.

Mike   Align behind your strong tackle. You have basically the 2 hole, but since the offense can't get a blocker off on you, you support anywhere and be ready to tackle vaulting ball carrier. On pass show you will be playing Banjo with your Strong Safety. You have the inside routes of #2 or #3. If #2 aligns wider, the Banjo is off and you have #3 man.

W.T.   Same as S.T.

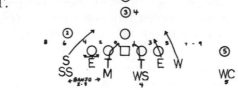

Diagram 317.

W.E.   Same as versus 22 Tight.

Will   Same as versus 22 Tight.

S.C.   #1 man "Me" call.

S.S.   Align head up #2. If he blocks, support in the 8 hole. If he releases, you are playing a Banjo with Mike. This means you have the outside route of #2 or #3. If #2 aligns wider, call off Banjo and play #2 man for man.

W.S.   Align behind your W.T. in a stack. Your first run responsibility is the 3 hole, but you are like Mike and can get to the ball without blocker interference. On pass show you are playing a Combo with your W.C. on #4 and #5. This is because #4 and #5 are close. It means you have the inside route of #4 or #5.

W.C.   Same as versus 22 Tight.

4. 65 versus 32 Flanker Split (Diagram #318).

Sam   Same as versus 22 Tight. If #2 (the tight end) flexes, you still have the 6 hole but also have the option of beating him back to the inside. Your angle must be upfield and you must get penetration. Another plan is for your Strong Safety to give you the 8 hole and take the 6 hole himself.

S.E.   Same as versus 22 Tight.

S.T.   Same as versus 22 Tight.

Mike   Stack with your Strong Tackle. Play is the same as described versus 31 I Slot. Again you are playing a Banjo with your Strong Safety on #2 and #3. There is no way you can cover #3 without getting picked off by #2.

W.T.   Same as versus 22 Tight.

W.E.   Everything is the same as described in 22 Tight. There is always a possibility of a TX with Will if he calls it.

Will   Same as 22 Flanker Split. There is one recognition problem. When our W.S. is stacked and there is a split end your side, you should be able to break off your charge and cover a quick flare to #4. It isn't hard to do because you are keying him anyway and would be giving to the outside at the first wide movements from #4. This is only block protection. This moves you in the right direction to cover the flare.

S.C.   Key and cover #1 man "Me" call.

S.S.   Align on #2. If #2 flexes, help Sam. This is a "Me" call. If #2 blocks, take 6 or 8 hole depending on what you told Sam to do. If #2 releases, you are playing Banjo with Mike on #2 and #3.

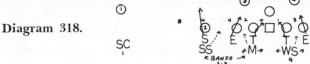

Diagram 318.

W.S.   Align behind your W.T. but shade to #4 just a little. Run support as described before. On pass show you have #4 man. Will will help on flares. You have to hustle on pass show to cover #4 on all other routes. Just remember, you can sprint to get leverage back, without fear of #4 setting you up wide then ducking back inside. The reason you should get help back to your inside is, that if the offense releases #4, they have to bring #3 back weak to block our Will. If they do that, they have to keep their tight end in to block Sam. When Mike realizes that #3 went weak and #2 blocks, he will come weak himself and can help on #4 inside.

W.C.   Align, key, and cover #5 "Me" call.

5. 65 versus 31 Strong Twins (Diagram #319).

Sam   Align in the same place you would if there were a tight end. Come hard on snap, keying the ball and #3. You are the container and must force the QB on all options. Chase contain plays away. You have 6 and 8 hole with help from Mike.

S.E.   Align almost head on the offensive tackle. On snap come hard through the tackle's outside knee. You have 4 hole responsibility.

S.T.   Same as versus 22 Tight.

Mike   Stack behind your S.T. You have 2 hole first, but can back up any P.O.A. On pass show you have #3 man for man.

W.T.   Same as versus 22 Tight.

W.E.   Same as versus 22 Tight.

Will   Same as versus 22 Tight.

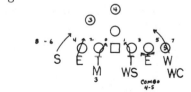

Diagram 319.

S.C.   Align on #1 three yards from the LOS. This is a "You" call because you are playing Combo on #1 and #2 with your S.S.

S.S.   Align on #2 two yards from the LOS. This is a "You" call because you are playing Combo with your S.C.

W.S.   Align behind your W.T., and key #4. Any release by #4 and #5 to the weak side creates a Combo between you and your W.C. You have any inside route. In this case it would be the weak tight end. Versus run you are a linebacker with 3 hole responsibility first. If #4 blocks, or goes strong, and pass shows you must help out on #5 running a short across a quick inside look in. This is part of your Combo with your W.C.

W.C.   Align just outside of #5. Normally you would be wider, but the set indicates the offense can't run wide too well to the weak side. Key #4 and #5. This is a Combo and you have all outside routes on pass show. Your W.S. should have any inside route by #5. Versus run your side, you have 9 hole responsibility.

6. 65 versus 32 Trips (Diagram #320).

Sam   This is a check to Fire 2. Align on #3. Key him for run or pass. Versus run you have the 6 hole. If he releases off on a run, the offense hasn't got a play, so when he releases cover him man for man.

S.E.   Align outside the offensive tackle because Sam will tell you he is "off." Use upright 2 point stance. Key the offensive tackle and the ball. Since this is Fire 2 and Mike will be firing the 2 hole, you take an outside route and the 4 hole. Contain and chase.

S.T.   Stunt with Mike. 0 hole responsibility.

Mike   Align over center as you can't stack this formation. Your W.S. is too wide for stacks. Check the defense to Fire 2 because Sam is the only one who can cover #3. Stunt with your Strong Tackle.

W.T.   When you hear the check to Fire 2 and Mike calls the other tackle's name, you know to use a spy technique. You have the 1 and 3 holes.

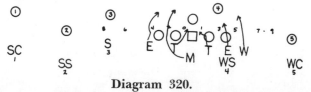

Diagram 320.

W.E.   Same as versus 22 Flanker Split.

Will   Same as versus 22 Flanker Split.

S.C.   Align on #1 2 yards from LOS and cover him man unless S.S. calls a Combo. If it is man coverage, it is a "Me" call. If it is Combo, it is a "You" call. On "You" call you have 8 hole responsibility.

S.S.   Align on #2, three yards from LOS. If #1 and #2 are more than 6 yards apart, call the number call indicating man coverage. You will have #2 man for man, and a "Me" call for 8 hole responsibility. If #1 and #2 are 6 yards or less, call Combo and a "You" call.

W.S.   Align just outside of #4. You have him man for man and the 9 hole for run support.

W.C.   Align on #5-man coverage.

Naturally, this is an unlikely set on the goal line. Run strength is not present and pass protection would be a problem.

This covers the alignments and techniques on 65, our defense for normal goal line situations. There is one other area of our upfield rules that must now change, and that is motion coverage. Down in this area we don't want to play zone. We also don't ever want to move Mike out of the middle, or take Sam or Will off of the blitz. With those thoughts in mind, here are our motion rules for our 65 defense.

Remember we covered earlier that all motions broke down into three categories, Cross Motion which changes strength, Strong Motion which does not change strength, and Counter Motion which is motion away from strength but still doesn't change strength. Basically what we are going to do is shuffle our Safeties and expand our corners. Let's keep in mind that only one kind of motion (Cross Motion) changes strength.

First, let's cover Counter Motion because it is the easiest of all.

1. Counter Motion to a split end (Diagram #321).

There is no problem here. Our W.S. has #4 man. When he goes in Counter Motion our W.S. just goes with him because #4 is his man anyway.

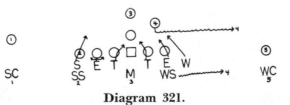

Diagram 321.

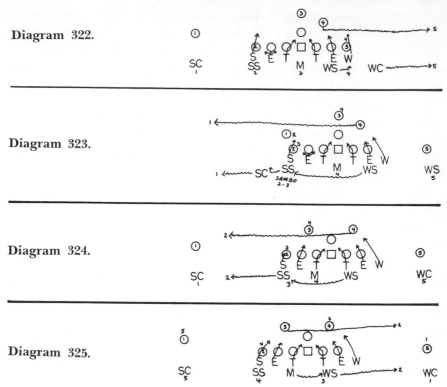

Diagram 322.

Diagram 323.

Diagram 324.

Diagram 325.

2. Counter Motion to a tight end (Diagram #322).

Here again this is no sweat. When #4 goes in counter motion outside of #5, then #4 becomes #5 and #5 becomes #4. Our W.C. expands with the motion man because he is #5. Our W.S. comes over and gets head up the Weak Tight End because he is now #4 and our W.S. covers him on passes.

3. Strong motion to a Tight Set (Diagram #323).

Our S.C. expands because corners always cover the widest eligible their side. The motion man (who was #4 now becomes #1). The close wing and tight end were #1 and #2, they now become #2 and #3. Our W.S. saw his man (#4) go in motion strong. He now knows he must shuffle to the strong side. He and the Strong Safety now play a Sambo on #2 and #3. This is what they would do upfield, they are just aligned closer to the LOS.

4. Strong motion to a wide flanker (Diagram #324).

This merely creates twins to our strong side. Our Strong Safety shuffles out with the motion because he knows he always goes out with twins. He also knows that #4 has become #2. Our W.S. sees his man (#4) go strong. He knows that he must shuffle strong. There is only one receiver left. Our W.S. has seen our S.S. go out with the motion so he (the W.S.) takes the remaining eligible which in this case was #2 (now #3) and was the S.S. man. So our W.S. takes the S.S. rules.

5. Cross motion to a split end (Diagram #325).

Cross motion is the toughest because all four secondary men must shift mental gears and count the eligibles from the opposite sides. It also means that our W.C. and W.S. become our S.C. and S.S. and that our S.C. and S.S. become our W.C. and W.S.

It isn't as tough as it sounds. Our W.C. still covers the widest eligible no matter what his number is. And our W.S. knows he has to go with motion to a split end, so even though the numbers change from #4 and #5 to #1 and #2, the rules still apply. Our S.S. would normally be on a Banjo with Mike on #2 and #3. However, when #3 went weak he knows the eligible in front of him is now #4 and he is now W.S. and the W.S. always covers #4. But even if he didn't figure out the number change he would still cover the tight end on passes. Mike, who was stacked, and playing Banjo, sees #3 go in motion weak. This tells him the remaining back is #3. He now has to come back to his middle position because the W.S. left. Mike also knows he has #3 now, even though his position is not too good. However, the offense simply cannot run a back off in long motion and release the remaining back without getting their passer killed. They could screen but Mike can cover a screen from where he is.

6. Cross Motion to a Tight End (Diagram #326).

First, our W.C. knows he has the widest eligible his side so he shuffles out with him. Our W.S. must come over and get head up the tight end. The tight end is now #2 and our W.S. is now our S.S. who covers #2. But even if he didn't understand the number switch, he would still know to cover the weak tight end if there were any motion to a weak tight end. Mike knows he must come back head up the center and cover #3. Our S.S. knows #2 went in motion weak and he must cover either back out of the I that might come his way.

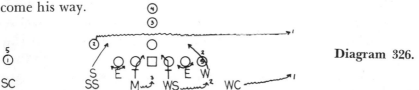

Diagram 326.

To sum up motion on the goal line, the idea is for our corners to always cover the widest eligibles on their side. The Safeties always cover the next widest eligible their side. If the second widest eligible goes in motion the other way, the affected safety must switch sides— if there isn't a second widest eligible left to cover. If the motion created twins, we cover that like we'd cover twins anywhere else. Our W.S. knows he must always go with motion to a split end. He also knows if the motion is to a tight end then he must cover the tight end. Mike, Will and Sam are not affected by motion on the goal line. Mike may have to come off of a stack, but he can see his W.S. leaving, so that is the logical thing to do. Mike also knows that any time the Banjo is off, he reverts to #3 man. Mike never leaves the middle.

This covers the 65 defensive rules and techniques. There are a few more things about goal line defense that should be brought out. I mentioned that defense in depth has been squashed down to a point where all the secondary people are linebackers. Add to that the descriptive word "Frenzy." One heck of a lot of mistakes can be overcome if the players are playing in a state of frenzy. Sometimes we describe this as imagining that the goal line is a cliff a mile high, and we are on the top and backed up to the edge. This will make the secondary people realize that lining up, or tackling, behind the goal line is no good. Confidence is essential because it makes our players *believe* that they will stop the offense. There is one more word that fits into this pattern. I don't like the word, but it's the only word that fits. That word is "luck." Of course, luck is part of belief. We have a saying among our defensive troops that if we can stop them three times, God will stop them once. Really, this is true. Defensively, you must figure that a certain percentage of the time the offense will stop themselves.

Now, let's summarize the whole ball of wax on goal line defense. First, a sound plan, well practiced. Second, a high degree of Frenzy. Third, Belief, and this includes the idea that somewhere along the line the offense will hurt its own chances. Belief isn't easy to sell, but you, as the coach, can sell success a lot better if you believe yourself. Most coaches, when somebody gets on their goal line, think "Oh My God, we are going to get scored on." Instead of this, you've got to let everyone know that they aren't going to score. If you run up and down, throwing a fit hollering "They won't score"—and they do; everyone will forget it anyway. But just as sure as you are afraid they might—my friend—they will.

12

Coaching the Goal Line—Short Yards

In the past two chapters we have covered long yards situations in the goal line area, and normal goal line defense. Now we come to the place where we must defend just two yards or less. We call this defense 65 Goal Line. It makes no difference what the down is, as long as there are two yards or less to go, we are going to defend this little area differently. I suppose there is one exception, but it is a rare one. In the case where the offense started on the two, and has had three cracks at us, and still hasn't scored, we would loosen up our pass defenders a bit. In this situation we would face a field goal attempt most of the time. However, there are times, due to time left in the game, and score, when a field goal wouldn't do the offense any good. In this rare case, we would go back to 65.

Our aims in this area of the field are to gamble that the offense won't throw the ball. If they do, we aren't necessarily beat. They have to get it off, and catch it, and we will still read releases and have a chance of covering it. But we are really thinking run—at least up to fourth and two. On fourth and less than a yard, we are still thinking run. Our interior people are going for the down and up charge with everyone taking the inside gap. Our corners are on the L.O.S. We are in a 92. Our Mike and Weak Safety have a real job to do. Everything that is done, must be done going forward. Mike and the Weak Safety must make square tackles and must back each other up to prevent spin offs. Here is 65 Goal line against a variety of sets that are plausible on the two-yard line.

1. 65 Goal Line vs. 22 Tight (Diagram #327).

Sam   Align head up the offensive tight end in a four point stance. On the snap charge the 4 hole. Use a down and

Diagram 327.

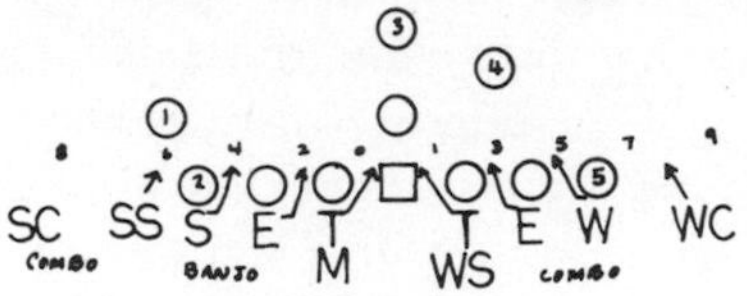

up technique. That is bending your elbows so that your shoulders are lower than your hips. When you charge, you drive down into the gap first landing on your hands while digging with your feet. While your feet are still digging you push up off of your hands and now drive up. It is like ricocheting off of the ground. The purpose is to get underneath the blocker's shoulders without burying your head. You can now see enough to make body adjustments and tackle. But even if you can't tackle, you want to make piles on the opponent's side of the L.O.S. If your outside blocker releases, come square up field and contain the passer. There is one more point in this area. Sam and Will do not flip-flop (that is align Sam strong, Will weak). Sam always plays left end and Will always plays right end. The reason for this is that flopping would be at a disadvantage if the offense went on a quick count. We will still align Mike strong and our Weak Safety weak. Also our Strong Safety must align on the strong side, but Sam and Will should be down in their stances ready to go when the offense breaks the huddle.

S.E.   Align head up the offensive tackle. On snap charge the 2 hole. Use the same techniques as described above for Sam. Quickness and penetration are mandatory. You should drive off of your outside foot stepping with your inside foot so that you will hit the hole square.

S.T.   Align head up the offensive guard. On snap, charge the 0 hole. Use the down-and-up technique described above. Your first thought is to secure the sneak, so you won't hit the hole as square as our ends. You want to take a piece of the center with you. With both our tackles pinching, the center will never get off to block on Mike or our W.S.

Mike   Align behind your S.T. Don't get tangled up in his feet. There are no open holes so all you have to do is find the ball and tackle the ball carrier square. On pass show you have the inside area your side.

W.T.   Same as our S.T. (1 hole).
W.E.   Same as our S.E. (3 hole).
Will   Same as Sam (5 hole).

S.C. Align on the line of scrimmage two yards outside of widest eligible. Key #1 and #2 on this set. If they both block, come hard upfield and take the 8 hole. Set square after three steps and stay square to the L.O.S. Meet inside out block with inside shoulder and flipper. Keep outside leg free. Don't get blocked out of 8 hole, force ball carrier deep. If either #1 or #2 release, play the outside route.

S.S. Align two yards from Sam on the L.O.S. Key #1. If he blocks, he will be blocking on you. Meet him with your outside leg and flipper and don't get caved in, making the 8 hole too big to close. Shed the blocker and bore into the 6 hole. If #1 releases they have no running play at you. Back up and cover any eligible between your corner and Mike. What you are really playing on this tight a set is Combo with your S.C. and Banjo with Mike.

W.S. Align behind your W.T. Your rules are the same as Mikes. You are playing a Combo with your W.C. on passes.

W.C. Align two yards from Will on the L.O.S. Key #5. If he blocks, support the 7 and 9 hole as your S.C. did on his side with a run key. If #5 releases, play Combo with your W.S. on #4 and #5.

2. 65 Goal Line versus 22 Flanker Split (Diagram #328).

Sam Same as versus 22 Tight.

S.E. Same as versus 22 Tight.

S.T. Same as versus 22 Tight.

Mike Same as versus 22 Tight, but you are definitely playing a Banjo with your S.S. on #2 and #3 on pass show.

W.T. Same as versus 22 Tight.

W.E. Same as versus 22 Tight.

Will Align where you would if the weak end were tight. Come hard on the snap, but don't get deeper than the ball as you must force options right away. Key #4 as he is the only one who can block on you. Read him for an inside-out block or an outside-in block. Keep your outside leg free, but limit the 5 hole. Force ball carrier deep. If #4 releases, get the passer down. If #4 goes away, chase.

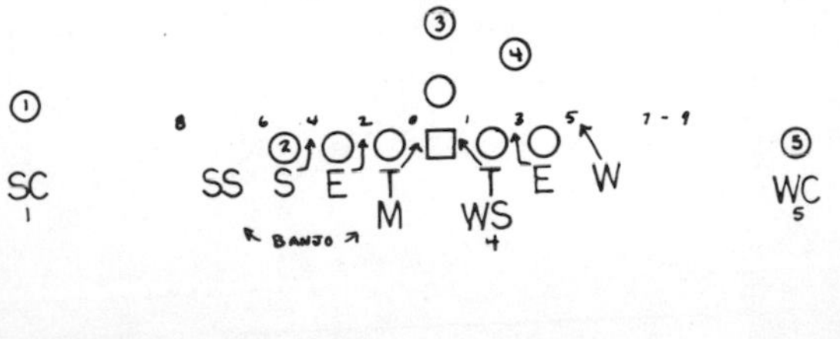

Diagram 328.

S.C.   Align on #1. Give him a two-yard cushion. Don't try to bump him. The bump off will give him just enough edge to catch the ball. Back pedal with him, break with him and watch his reaction for the ball. You must not take your eyes off of #1. You may sense a run, but you can't support until all threat of a pass is gone. On the two-yard line that means you are out of the run. Beware of the "pick" pass where #1 cracks back on your S.S. and the tight end releases outside. You will have to cover #1 as he goes inside but, since your SS is on the line, #1 route is too flat for a look in. Holler "Crack" and pick up #2.

S.S.   Align two yards from Sam on the L.O.S. Key #2. If he blocks, support the run as described for our S.C. versus 22 Tight when he got a run key. You are not charging on the snap. You are keying so you will see a quick, phony block by #2 and be able to pick him up if he releases. If, on this situation, you hear "Crack" from your S.C., turn to the outside and deck #1 coming back in on you. Any release by #2 creates a Banjo and you have the outside route of #2 and #3.

W.S.   Same as versus 22 Tight except that you have #4 man on pass show. Handle the "pick pass" the same as described above for our S.C. and S.S.

W.C.   Same as S.C. Key #5 and play as described for our S.C. on #1.

Every set that is tight, such as the power I or dead T would be played the same as described versus 22 Tight. Any set featuring wide-outs would be handled the same way as described versus 22 Flanker Split. For exact alignments and motion coverage see the preceding chapter. Everything we did there can be applied to Goal line 65. The main difference is that Sam and Will are charging inside tight ends. Our Corners are on the line as is our S.S.

20 GOAL LINE DO'S AND DON'TS

1. Do drive blockers into the POA.
2. Don't pursue until you've insured your assignment.
3. Do upset timing by penetration.
4. Don't be in a hurry to do something if you are the outside men.
5. Do keep back side chase angle on the ball.
6. Don't let one man make the tackle, avoid spin offs.

7. Do lay your ears back and come hard.
8. Don't get "caved in" when gap charging.
9. Do bounce in place, linebackers, if not sure of POA.
10. Don't cross the center fast, linebackers.
11. Do keep your shoulders parallel to the L.O.S.
12. Don't turn inside to meet blockers, outside men.
13. Do get under blocker's shoulders, inside men.
14. Don't take your eyes off of a wide-out when you are one on one.
15. Do force the option immediately.
16. Don't bump wide receiver when you are covering one on one.
17. Do know the offense's goal line tendencies.
18. Don't let offensive linemen split you out, take the gap.
19. Do get the hair up on the back of your neck.
20. Don't stay blocked.

A final word from the author. As I look back over this vast stack of defensive notes, I feel that I would like to leave the reader with one last coaching point. A parting shot, so to speak.

Of all the things that are important in this great game of football, the most important thing you can impart to your players is the ability to meet adversity and come back tough with a hard nose. We are living in an age when young people question the value of authority and discipline. They question why they must be trained to meet adversity of any kind. Many of them come apart like a wet cookie at the first sign of responsibility. They think happiness is doing their thing; which in reality is *no* thing. In football they can learn that happiness is pride in what you have earned. Twice the happiness is felt when unusual obstacles or adversities have been overcome. So I close this book with the wish that coaches everywhere will continue to help young men find the answer to future happiness by being a team man that has earned his own way, and recovered from minor setbacks with a stronger purpose and a harder nose.

Index